Money doesn't grow on trees?!

The Indispensable Guide to Simple and Secure Money Management

Christopher D. Hudson
Katie D. Gieser
Timothy Baker
Christine Collard Erickson
David A. Jennings
Carol Smith
Len Woods

BARBOUR
PUBLISHING

Produced with the assistance of the Livingstone Corporation (www.Livingstonecorp.com). Project staff
includes Christopher D. Hudson, Ashley Taylor, Rosalie Krusemark, and Greg Longbons.

Interior and cover design by Karen Cassel Bear.

Cover artwork by Veer.

Published by Barbour Publishing, Inc., P.O. Box 719, Uhrichsville, Ohio 44683,
www.barbourbooks.com

*Our mission is to publish and distribute inspirational products offering exceptional value and biblical encourage-
ment to the masses.*

Member of the
Evangelical Christian
Publishers Association

Printed in the United States of America.
5 4 3 2 1

TABLE OF CONTENTS

13 Insurance 161

14 Retirement 173

15 Glossary 185

16 Resources for Further Enlightenment 187

Wouldn't it be nice if money grew on trees? As much as we'd wish otherwise, money unfortunately plays a large role in our lives—what we plan to do today, next week, and ten years from now, and how we'll do those things, too.

Whether it's harnessing seemingly uncontrollable debt, knowing how to get Junior through college, or, most importantly, learning to be a good steward of the resources the Lord has given you, getting a handle on your finances is a big deal. Help is not far away. . .you're actually holding it right now!

The think tank at *The Indispensable Guide* headquarters has pulled together a wide array of topics, placing themselves at your disposal for your monetary needs (theoretical or emotional, that is, not cold cash!). There's a wealth (no pun intended) of information in this fine volume on just about anything you could think to do with money—from spending it, to saving it, to talking to your kids about it, to hopefully someday retiring with some of it. More specifically, you'll find. . .

A Truckload of Clues

You'll learn tips and ideas from people who don't necessarily have a lot of money but who are learning to successfully manage what they do have.

Perspective

We easily get caught up in the web money can spin around us. To live more peacefully and securely, though, we sometimes need help looking at the big picture. We'll help you take a step back.

Amazing Stories and Facts

Dealing with those greenbacks can produce some fascinating stories and interesting facts. We've collected a few choice pieces for you to enjoy.

Important Reminders

Certain things are important to remember as you endeavor to manage your money. We've highlighted those for you.

The Bottom Line

We'll help you get beyond confusion by letting you know the most important stuff to remember.

Help from Above

We've highlighted a few key verses that will help you understand what God has to say about money.

Before you break that piggy bank, read this book! It has all kinds of things to say about you and your money, like how to get the most out of the change rattling around in that pink pig. Feel free to read it your way: from cover to cover or skipping around to the parts that interest you most. No matter how you read it, you'll find it's jammed with good advice, great ideas, and entertaining thoughts. So turn the page and start reading. . .you'll be glad you did!

Money 101

Welcome to the Great Tug-o'-War!

You're sitting at the kitchen table. You know the drill. Sit for hours. Pay the bills. Try and manage the family money.

The system is simple. Write a check. Check your balance and see if you can write another one. Write another check. And then another. When it's finally over, you've got several stacks. Bills you've paid. . .waiting to be mailed. Bills you couldn't pay this time. *Maybe next paycheck*, you think to yourself. *I hope they don't call this time.*

Ahh, it's over. You're walking away when your spouse enters the kitchen. "Oh, good," she says. "I hope you remembered to pay the dentist this month. They called me at work today asking for the money we owe." *Oh, great,* you think. So, it's back to the table for the money juggle that you've become very adept at.

Money

Depending on who you are, what you make, where you live, how high your self-esteem is, and a variety of other factors, money can either empower you or strangle you. Have too little money, and that factor alone can bring out other possibly critical flaws. Have too much and a totally different set of problems arises. We want this book to help you begin getting control over the money in your life. No one should have to navigate the money maze alone. We're here to help!

De Powah of Cash!

A lot of things have power in our society, but few can match the power of money in your life. Here's your chance to think through the power that money has. In the space below, write some of the things that money has the power to do, change, or create.

_____

_____

Okay, you've made your list; we'd like to share our list with you. Here are some more things that we think money has the power to do:

❀ It has the power to provide for you: When you have money, you can buy stuff.

❀ It has the power to provide for others: When you have money, you can buy stuff for others. You can also help others out of financial binds.

❀ It helps provide security: Money might help you feel secure.

❀ It fills in the gaps: Money provides for us the stuff that we need (food and clothing) and gets us stuff that we want (a new Porsche, the latest home video game, nice hair bows).

Okay, all of that is nice. But let's be real for a moment. Money has personal power, as well. Whatever changes it makes in society or in the lives of other people is nice. But in reality, you're probably more concerned about money in *your* life (unless you're reading this book for someone else).

What kind of power does money have in your life? This is the part of the book that we can't write for you. We'd like you to think about how much power money has in your life. Think through the following questions and write your answers after each question.

❀ How much do I depend on money? What do I depend on it to do?

_____

❀ How much money do I think I need to have to live?

_____

❀ What should I do with money I have that's extra? Invest it? Give it? Save it? Why?

_____

❀ How much debt do I feel is reasonable?

_____

❀ How do I feel God views the money I have? What does He think about the way I use the money He gives me?

_____

❀ How much money should I have set aside for my children's college, my retirement, or for surprise expenses?

_____

Getting a realistic focus on how powerful money is in your life is essential for grasping what we're serving up in this book. We want you to organize and enhance your use of money and remove the despair the money issue might cause you to feel. You've just accomplished an incredible first step in getting an understanding of the money in your life. Now, let's step back and look at the big picture for a moment.

God and Your Cash

Let's dive into a few ideas. Here are a few things that, while they're easy to believe, aren't true:

❀ God gives people He loves more money.

❀ People who've done something wrong will become poor.

❀ God loves rich people more than poor people—or vice versa.

❀ Rich people are happier than poor people.

❀ Money is divine. It has a conscience. It cares about you.

Cracking open this book comes with a price. "What's the price?" you ask. Well, it's simple. We want you to have a new focus on your money. And it all begins with one simple (but not new) concept.

God

Okay, so you're not startled by this revelation. Consider, though, that everything you have comes from God. So, take a moment to list everything you own.

_____

_____

So you know what you've got. Now, how do you put all of that into perspective?

First, remember that God gave us everything that we have: the car we drive, the house we live in, the food we eat. You get the point. Because of His love for us, God has provided the things we need to live, and even some things that we don't need but would make us happy (that extra-nice bedroom ensemble, for example). So when you look at the things you have, remember that they're there because of God's love for you.

Second, while it's easy to look at the things God has given us and begin worshiping them, that's not what God wants. Here's where it's really important to draw a very distinct line in the sand. When God provides us with things, He desires that we take good care of them. For example, it's a good idea to take care of our car with regular checkups, or have our carpets cleaned occasionally.

Priorities

For an instant lesson on your own personal priorities, look over the list you've made under the subhead "God," and begin prioritizing this stuff. Write the number "1" next to the most important thing on that list. Then continue numbering until all of these things have been numbered. There! You just got a snapshot of what's most important to you.

However, when God provides really cool things, it's easy to worship those things. When God provides a new car, for example, we sometimes tend to obsess about the cleanliness of the car. Or, when we're able to buy our dream house, we might tend to not allow normal living to occur (for example, not allowing people into the living room because we don't want the carpet messed up). However, when we do this, we actually end up worshiping those things above God. And when we honor a thing above God, we're in a really bad place.

So, when God provides, it's important to remember that God's gifts aren't things to be worshiped. They are to be enjoyed.

The Ultimate Use

Once we've got a correct perspective on our money, how should we use it? Consider what God's Word directs us to do.

> *If anyone has material possessions and sees his brother in need but has no pity on him, how can the love of God be in him?*
>
> 1 John 3:17

What does this passage say? It's pretty clear. One basic and important understanding about money is the giving factor. God has designed an almost mathematical process whereby the following is true: God provides—we're asked to be good stewards—as a result of being good stewards, we notice people who are in need—we give to needs as God directs, out of the excess He's given. And, while all of that might be an oversimplification, the truth is that God calls all of us to give out of what He's given to us.

Ending the Cash-Coaster

So, everything financial is out of control in your life. The cards are maxed.

The savings are spent. And, even though you've got plenty of checks left, the bank says you're out of money. Since we're about to lay out a lot of information in this book, we'd like to give you some steps for managing your out-of-control situation.

Giving up spiritual control

It's often-quoted advice, but less often followed, that in order for things to be straight in your life, you've got to give God control. But it's still true—and especially in this area. Want to get control of your financial situation? Spend significant time asking God to take control of it.

Giving up physical control

You might not like it, but getting control of how you spend, or how you manage, your finances might mean asking someone to help you. That might not be easy because we feel like finances are a private and personal matter. But sometimes it helps to have someone else's perspective on how we budget and spend. Look for someone you really trust (like a close friend) or a certified financial counselor.

So you're ready to dive into this book. You're ready to climb the money mountain and take control, save some money, educate your children, and even let your money work for you. Before you head for the next chapter, take a moment to evaluate yourself and your view of money.

I feel like I have a healthy grasp on the money in my life.
AGREE. . . . . DISAGREE

In my opinion, I am not too dependent on the money in my life.
AGREE. . . . . DISAGREE

I believe that God provides me with the money I need.
AGREE. . . . . DISAGREE

I have a healthy plan for saving money.
AGREE. . . . . DISAGREE

In general, I have control of my money.
AGREE. . . . . DISAGREE

Hi! Read Me.

Navigating through the money maze isn't easy. But you can do it! The pages of this book are filled with helpful ideas, advice, and tips all aimed at getting you through the money maze successfully. Here's what you'll find in the pages ahead.

Budgets

You love 'em. You hate 'em. You need 'em! Although budgets might feel totally impossible to create and live by, they're totally necessary for navigating through the money maze. You'll find real advice, tried and proven steps to create your own budget, and how to make it work in your life.

Tithing

If you have difficulty letting go of your cash, these pages will help you. You'll get a picture of God's perspective on our stuff. If you find tithing difficult, you'll find encouragement here.

Saving

Never have enough for those unexpected car problems? Worried that your kids will need emergency dental treatment and you've got no idea how to pay for it? Saving might be your answer. These pages will help you set up a plan for regular saving. That includes ideas for where to put your money, whom to trust with it, what to spend savings on, and a host of other ideas.

Investing

You can make a lot of money in the market. You could also lose everything. One thing's for sure: If you don't try, you'll never know. Beginning might just be the most difficult part of investing. These pages will jump-start you in the wonderful world of investing.

Money and Your Children

You know a lot about finances, but you're perplexed about how to pass on those ideas. Or you're worried that your kids will live out your financial blunders. This section will arm you with real advice for passing on solid financial tools to your kids.

Education

Whatever you paid for your post-high-school education, your kids will pay double. This section will help you learn how to budget, plan, and prepare for your children's education.

A TRUCKLOAD OF CLUES

The Right Approach

As you read through this book, remember there are a number of approaches you might want to take as you attack this resource:

- Consider reading the sections that apply to your situation. If you're short on time, look for ideas that speak to your situation and brainstorm ideas for applying them to your life.

- Begin at the beginning and read it straight through. As you read, consider marking up the book so you'll be able to read over sections at a later time and apply what you've highlighted.

- We've made this book interactive, so you might want to get together with a study group and work through sections or concepts together. As you do this, keep each other accountable for ideas that you've committed to try in your lives.

Purchasing

What's the best way to buy stuff? Coupons? Credit cards? And how do you know if you really need to buy something? In this section you'll get real tools for using your money wisely.

Debt Management

It's so easy to get deeply in debt, and it's so difficult to climb out of the pit that credit leads you into. In this section, you'll work through issues like how to get out of debt, how to avoid bankruptcy, and how to consolidate your debt.

Loans

So, you want to buy a home, but you're clueless where to start. This section will help you get started in your thinking about home buying.

Rent/Mortgages

Striking a difference between owning and renting isn't always easy. Is it always better to buy a home instead of rent? This section will help you understand the pros and cons of both renting and buying a home.

Taxes

It's important to obey the law. But what does the law allow you to do with your money? What are the most beneficial ways to manage stocks and savings? This section will give you understanding into the wide world of taxes.

Insurance

Do you need renter's insurance? Should you get whole life or term life insurance? What's the best deductible to have? This section will help you find your way through the insurance maze.

Retirement

It's not as easy as it used to be. Work hard your whole life, then sit back and enjoy your golden years. Well, not anymore. . .unless you're careful. This section will help you understand what you need to do now so you can retire when the time is right.

Glossary

What's the difference between a growth stock and an income stock? You can spell *annuity*, but do you know what it is? This section defines some difficult financial words.

Resources for Further Enlightenment

You love this book, but you're not finished learning about money. These ideas will help you take the next step in your money education.

Budgets

Benefits of a Budget

The Lost Art of "Fiscal Discipline"

An extraterrestrial visitor would discover some interesting things about us earthlings. A perusal of one of our Sunday newspapers (overflowing with advertising!) would reveal that we are a race of consumers, that commerce and purchasing are among our chief priorities in life. If this stranger beamed itself into one of our shopping malls, he/she/it would assume that we humans have an inordinate need to acquire unlimited quantities of goods and services. E.T. would ponder the power of the small, colorful, plastic cards we earthlings routinely whip from our wallets and purses and use to get more and more and more stuff.

What all this translates into on a *personal* level is the highest consumer debt in the history of planet Earth. Personal bankruptcies are at record levels (and increasing annually).

In short, most people are spending far more money than they are earning. And why not? Our own federal government does it. Gone is the concept of "fiscal discipline." Forget the notion of "living within our means." Despite the political rhetoric (especially in election years), any honest bean counter will tell you that we haven't had a *true* balanced budget in years. This cavalier approach to money and spending was captured years ago in the words of one loose-lipped lawmaker, "A billion dollars here, a billion dollars there—pretty soon you're talking about some serious money."

AMAZING STORIES AND FACTS

Sophie Says:

"I've been rich and I've been poor. Rich is better."
—Sophie Tucker

What is needed? What is the solution for people gripped by out-of-control spending habits?

The Simple Concept of Budgeting

Budget. To many this word is odious or hateful. It sounds oppressive and restrictive. After all, who wants to be "enslaved" by financial boundaries?

But actually, a budget, when understood and implemented, can be quite liberating. It frees us from our culture's relentless pressure to buy everything we see. It frees us from the heavy burden of wondering how we are going to pay bills that far exceed our income. It frees us to be appreciative of all that God gives. It frees us from having to worry about creditors and collection agents, past-due notices, and bankruptcy proceedings.

The Simple Budget. . .a Helpful and Amazing Tool

A budget is nothing more than a giving/saving/spending plan. It's an accounting tool that, utilized correctly, keeps us accountable and has the power to make life much more enjoyable.

There are at least four advantages to budgeting:

1. *Putting yourself on a budget helps you see why you're in financial trouble and how you got there.*

   Once you begin tracking your actual day-to-day financial habits and comparing them to your plan (i.e., your budget), you'll see clearly where you are "hemorrhaging" economically. Without a budget, Bob and Carol would never realize why "there's too much month at the end of the money." However, once they commit to the process, they'll realize, among other things, the startling fact that between the two of them they're spending almost $400 per month dining out (plus another $300 per month on groceries)!

2. *A budget can help get you out of current financial trouble.*

   Problems don't typically fix themselves. They first have to be diagnosed; then a workable solution has to be devised. A well-crafted budget functions the same way. It's a remedy for financial malaise. It's medicine for those who are in economic ill health. But, of course, for the cure to work, the prescription must be taken. An unutilized budget does about as much good as an unopened vial of lifesaving medicine.

3. *A budget can help keep you out of future financial trouble.*

   If you are serious about wanting to be financially healthy, you have to grant your budget the authority to govern (and even have "veto" power over) your economic decisions. Consider:

   ❦ Donna is at the mall, and though she has already spent her clothing budget for the month (it's only the eighth), she finds a "darling" outfit—on sale! She rationalizes, "I know what. . .I'll just consider this as a clothing expense for *next month*!" Out comes the almost maxed-out MasterCard.

   ❦ Becca is deliberately transferring $100 from her checking account to her savings account (because that's what her budget calls for her to do each month). By doing this, her checking balance will be extremely low. She will now have to be super careful (payday is still ten days away!). But she gulps and carries out the transaction.

Of the two, who is really living by a budget? Of the two (if the trends continue), who is likely to end up in good financial shape?

AMAZING STORIES
AND FACTS

The Rule of 72

Invested money earns interest. And interest has a compounding effect, so that invested money grows. You can even use the "rule of 72" to determine how fast your money will double. This formula is simple. Just divide 72 by the interest rate your money is earning. Let's say at age twenty-two, you put $2,000 in a stock mutual fund. And let's say that the fund earns, during your working years, an average of 8 percent a year (historically the stock market has averaged, over the long haul, closer to 10 percent). Your $2,000 will double in nine years because 72 divided by 8 equals 9. So at age thirty-one, your investment, without your having added another penny, is suddenly worth $4,000.

By age forty, you've got $8,000. That doesn't sound like much, but watch as the compounding accelerates. At forty-nine, it's worth $16,000. At fifty-eight, $32,000. At age sixty-seven, you'd have $64,000—all from an initial $2,000 investment.

Now, suppose you had started saving earlier. Or imagine if you had disciplined yourself to save/invest some money, say $83 every month (i.e., $1,000 annually). Such an investment (beginning at age twenty-two, and averaging 12 percent) would be worth over $767,000 by age sixty-two!

4. A budget can help you reach financial goals/economic security.

We all admire the person who is in amazing shape. While a flawless physique is *occasionally* the result of sheer genetic good fortune, it is *normally* the result of long-term hard work and discipline.

This same phenomenon is true in the financial realm. A few folks are born with silver spoons in their mouths (and lots of bucks in their trust funds). But most people find financial success by devising a plan and then faithfully pursuing their economic goals. It's not magic and it's not rocket science. It's mostly common sense and plain old discipline.

The point? With almost no financial savvy—just lots of discipline—you could be wealthy at retirement. Or you could have $325 and a few dog-eared baseball cards in a shoe box. It's your call.

How to Set Up a Budget

Setting up a budget sounds worse and more complicated than it actually is. Think of it as a fiscal game, a monetary puzzle, a financial brainteaser. Then determine (with your spouse, if you're married) to solve this economic challenge. Millions of other people (most of them not nearly so bright as you!) have done it and are living joyfully within their means. If they can do it, so can you.

Follow these steps:

1. Pray.

Thank God for all the material blessings you have. If you need to, make a list. Remember that everything you own and everything you have (including your job) is a gift from Him (James 1:17). Ask God for wisdom to not only *survive* your economic trials, but to *thrive* in the midst of them (James 1:2–5). Trust Him to show you a workable plan that will not only honor Him, but bring financial freedom to you.

2. Get a legal pad and several sharpened pencils.

Draw a vertical line down the middle of the page. On the left side you will calculate your income. In the right column, you will devise a new budget. Use a pencil with a good eraser (no one correctly crafts a perfect budget on the first try!).

3. Determine your total inflow.

Before you know how much money you have available to give, save, and spend, you first have to know what your total income is. Salary, royalties, gifts, pay for part-time work or odd jobs, interest income, dividends, and investment profits—list these in the left-hand column of your legal pad, add them all up, and the result will be your gross income.

Note: It's probably wise not to include "iffy" income in this amount. For example, if you're *hoping* to get a $3,000 raise in a few months, but it's not a sure thing yet, use your current, lower figures to be on the safe side.

4. Determine an amount for tithes/gifts/charitable giving.

It's important to think of this first. Why? Not only does the Bible speak of the importance of giving to God as a *top priority*, but experience

Honor the Lord

HELP FROM ABOVE

God cares about your decisions. The Bible says: "Honor the Lord with your wealth, with the firstfruits of all your crops; then your barns will be filled to over-flowing, and your vats will brim over with new wine" (Proverbs 3:9–10).

shows that if we *wait* to give from what's left over, we'll probably never give because there is rarely anything left over!

Whether you give a tithe (i.e., one-tenth of your income —of either your gross or net) or whether you give *more* than 10 percent (or less) is between you and God (2 Corinthians 9:6–10). *But* the important thing to keep in mind is that God is the true *Owner* of all "our" stuff (Psalm 24:1; Haggai 2:8), and we're only supposed to be *managers* of it. This means we should constantly consult Him on how much of *His* money and stuff He wants us to give back to Him.

In the right-hand column (the "new budget" category) write down an amount that, with God's help, you'd like to begin giving monthly to your church, parachurch ministries, missionaries, etc. Determine, by the grace of God, to live up to this commitment.

5. Determine your tax liabilities.

Using last year's tax return or a recent paycheck stub, calculate how much of your gross income needs to be earmarked for the payment of federal taxes, state and local taxes (if any), and FICA. If you already have lots of money withheld from your paychecks, this will not be a factor for you. However, if you normally owe additional taxes at the end of the year, or if you are self-employed and required to pay taxes quarterly, this is a vital step.

Write these amounts in the right-hand column on your legal pad, under the amount designated for giving. Remember, taxes are not optional expenditures. Well, on second thought, you *could* opt not to pay them, but only if you want to relocate from your house to "the big house." This is not a wise move, nor a biblical one. Jesus instructed His followers to "give to Caesar what is Caesar's, and to God what is God's" (Matthew 22:21).

6. Determine your level of savings.

Next, in the column to the right, designate an amount (experts suggest anywhere from 5 to 10 percent) of your remaining income for *savings*. Like giving, this is an area generally ignored by most people until the very end of the budgeting process, at which point there's little or no money left to set aside for savings!

It takes enormous discipline to establish the savings habit. In an impatient culture where the majority of people want only to live for the moment and buy, buy, buy, it's tough to go against the flow and plan and prepare for one's future. But not to do so is the height of foolishness. At a minimum, you must think about retirement. If you're banking solely on Social Security to fund your golden years, you're kidding yourself. You'll need other supplemental income and savings to live comfortably. It's also wise to have six or eight months' income in a special *emergency savings fund*—money that you can get to easily if the need arises.

One good way to make this savings habit less painful is to set up a monthly bank draft whereby a certain amount of your paycheck is automatically (and immediately) deducted from your checking account into a money market or mutual fund. If you don't ever actually "have" this money in your checking account, it is easier to do without it.

Many discerning folks also plan for other long-term savings needs: future college or educational needs, orthodontia for the kids, cars, vacations, even upcoming Christmas spending. A general rule is "the more you can save, the better."

7. Determine your spendable income.

How? In the right-hand column, simply subtract your giving and taxes and savings from your gross income totals in the far left column. The total is what you have left to actually spend—and not a penny more (not if you want to avoid the terrible trap of debt).

Do not faint. Take a deep breath. You can do it. God can give you the wisdom to allocate this remaining money where it needs to go. He will meet all your needs (Philippians 4:19), though maybe not all your desires.

8. Set up the specific budget categories that fit your family.

No two families are exactly alike. The following is a sample list (that can spark your thinking). Not all the following categories will fit your situation, but copy the ones that do apply onto the right side of your legal pad:

PERSPECTIVE

Tools

"Money and possessions are a very effective tool God uses to grow us up. Therefore, we shouldn't ask, 'God, why are You doing this to me?' but 'God, what do You want me to learn?' "

—Ron Blue

Housing
 Mortgage (or rent)
 Insurance (homeowner's or renter's)
 Taxes
 Electricity
 Water
 Sanitation
 Gas
 Telephone
 Cable TV
 Repairs/maintenance
 Furnishings (appliances, furniture)
 Cleaning (supplies/services)
 Supplies (toilet paper, kitchen items, etc.)
 Lawn care/gardening
 Decorations (curtains, wall hangings, etc.)
 Pest control
 Other
Groceries
Automobile(s)
 Payments (loans/leases)
 Gas and oil
 Insurance
 License/taxes
 Maintenance/repair
 Other
Insurance
 Life
 Medical
 Disability
 Other
Debts
 Credit cards
 Loans (nonmortgage) and notes
 Other
Entertainment and Recreation
 Eating out
 Baby-sitters
 Activities/hobbies
 Vacations
 Club memberships
 Other

Clothing
Gifts
    Christmas
    Birthdays
    Anniversaries
    Other
Medical Expenses (out of pocket)
    Doctors
    Dentists
    Hospital
    Prescriptions
    Other
Personal Care
    Toiletries
    Beauty shop/barber
Miscellaneous
    Laundry
    Postage
    Subscriptions
    Pets
    Internet service
    Pocket money/allowances
Education
    Tuition
    Lunches
    Supplies
    Field trips/special programs
    Club fees

9. *Make an initial "guesstimate" of your current monthly expenses.*

Some expenses are hard to calculate because they vary from month to month. For example, in the summer, when you are traveling more (and fuel prices are higher), you may spend $125 a month on gasoline; whereas, in the fall, you may only spend $85 a month. Other expenses, however, do not vary from month to month. For instance, your rent or mortgage payment (if you have a fixed-rate loan) is a constant figure. Most college loans are also a fixed monthly rate.

Your best bet is to utilize old check registers and credit card receipts (if you have them) and begin to allocate your spendable income (gross income minus giving, taxes, and saving) to the various budget categories that fit your unique situation.

The goal here is to be realistic. Don't allocate extravagant sums, but also don't seriously "underfund" a budget category.

10. Add up your expenses.
Chances are you'll find that you've allocated more money for spending than you actually have in income. If so (and you're in debt), you now should have a good clue as to why you're in a financial hole.

11. Adjust your expenses by analzying and prioritizing.
Let's say your first budget attempt contains $300 more in expenses than you have income. This means you've got to go back and shave some spending. This takes guts, nerves, wisdom, right priorities, and a certain ruthlessness.

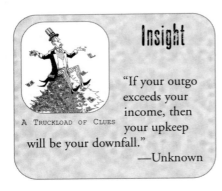

Insight

"If your outgo exceeds your income, then your upkeep will be your downfall."

—Unknown

A TRUCKLOAD OF CLUES

Sure, you'd love to continue spending $200 a month on new clothes (who wouldn't?)! But for your family's financial health, you may need to knock that figure down as low as $125. Could you save $10 monthly by shopping smarter at the grocery store and using coupons? How about another $5 per month by dropping those subscriptions for magazines you don't even have time to read?

A lot of little adjustments can add up to bring your budget into line. If, however, the gap between your income and spending is huge, you will have to consider some serious lifestyle changes. Perhaps you've taken on too large a mortgage. *The Indispensable Guide* editorial team knows numerous families who have opted to go against the flow and downsize. Was it a hard decision to move to a less expensive home? Sure. Was it easy to implement? No way. Are these families in better financial shape than before? You'd better believe it!

If you're *serious* about taking control of your finances (rather than letting them control you), you'll look hard at every category. Do you *really* need two brand-new automobiles and the high debt that often comes with them? Could you "get by" with one new car and find a good used car at half the price of the other new vehicle?

The point is to stay there hunched over your legal pad until the right-hand total equals the amount at the bottom of the left-hand column. That's called a balanced budget. That's a plan that will allow you to live within your means and avoid the stress that's destroying so many families (including millions of Christians).

How to Abide by a Budget

Setting up a budget is one thing; *living by* a budget is another. Planning a budget is an exercise a person or couple can complete in one afternoon or evening; carrying out your financial goals takes the rest of your life.

Some Reminders:

- A budget is really nothing more than a unique financial plan. It's a guide for how you sense God wants you to manage the assets He's placed in your care.
- A first budget represents your best guesstimate for what it will cost for you to live in a way that honors God. Realize you will have to adjust your budget from time to time to reflect changes in income or new expenses.
- Living within a budget means you don't spend more money than you have coming in. It's that simple.

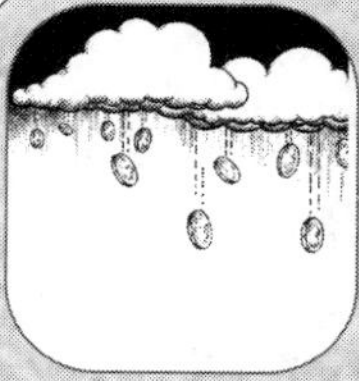

HELP FROM ABOVE

An Apple a Day. . .

God cares about your decisions. The Bible says: "The fruit of the Spirit is. . .self-control" (Galatians 5:22–23).

So, now that you've got a financial plan, how can you begin moving toward financial health?

Abiding by Your Budget

1. ***Seek help from above.***
   The indwelling Holy Spirit can give you the strength to say no to impulsive purchasing decisions. Not only this, He can give you the courage to "stay the course." Just because everyone else is trading in their car every third year doesn't mean you have to follow suit.

2. ***Pray about every financial decision.***
   Or at least ones involving expenditures of more than $25. This is a good habit because it forces you to remember that "your" stuff and "your" money is really God's. He's the Owner and you're the manager. One day we will all have to stand before the Lord and give an account for how we've lived, for how well (or poorly) we've utilized His gifts (2 Corinthians 5:9–10).

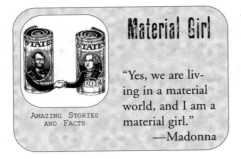

3. Sleep a night or two before every major financial decision.

It's interesting how irresistible that new tool or outfit seems when you first see it on display, and how unnecessary it often becomes after you've pondered and prayed about buying it for twenty-four to forty-eight hours. If you can learn to resist those first impulsive spending urges and pull back and get some perspective, you'll find yourself living

Lifestyle Changes

A TRUCKLOAD OF CLUES

"During our early years of marriage, my wife and I were living near and working in a very affluent community. The only problem was that *we* weren't affluent! All around us were gorgeous homes, expensive cars, and exclusive shops. Over time we noticed ourselves becoming more and more materialistic. We finally had to make some conscious lifestyle changes to combat this problem:

• We quit perusing all the mail-order catalogs that flooded our mailbox.

• We quit going to stores and malls to browse and window-shop (this only whetted our appetite for more things).

• We quit watching so much television (realizing that we were being subjected to hundreds of commercials designed solely to make us dissatisfied with our "stuff" and desirous of new "stuff").

• We made it a regular exercise to stop and "count our blessings." This switched our focus from "what do we *not* have" to "what God has blessed us with."

• We tried to focus more on giving and serving. We realized that generosity is the great antidote to greed. By holding our possessions and money with an open hand, they were less able to "grip our hearts."

—Walter, Atlanta, Georgia

On Guard!

HELP FROM ABOVE

God cares about your decisions. The Bible says: "Watch out! Be on your guard against all kinds of greed; a man's life does not consist in the abundance of his possessions" (Luke 12:15).

with less and enjoying it more.

4. *Avoid temptation.*

The best way for an alcoholic to keep from "falling off the wagon" is to steer clear of places that serve alcohol. The same is true for those who have a tendency to overspend and bust the budget. Don't put yourself in situations where your purchasing juices will get stirred up!

Budgets

5. *Cut up your credit cards (or cut back on your use of them).*

For many, a primary cause of debt and overspending is too much "plastic." Unless you're a penny-pincher with an iron will, carrying credit cards can be extremely dangerous. There's something so convenient and innocuous about pulling a VISA card out and making a "little" purchase. But those $10 and $25 acquisitions have a way of adding up. The pain and anguish (and debt) come when you get your statement.

Every financial counselor worth his or her salt will tell you to cut up your credit cards, unless you pay the account balance in full each month. And even if you don't carry a balance, studies prove that when we pay cash for things, we tend to spend less.

The general rule is this: Use credit cards only as a convenience. Never use them to pay for things you can't afford.

6. *Be willing to make lifestyle changes.*

Getting your financial house in order will require alterations in the way you live. If you are spending more than you are earning and you want this trend to stop, you only have two choices: Either stop spending so much or start earning more.

Many people, unwilling to put the brakes on their consumptive practices, choose the second option. But this isn't always the wisest course of action. When both parents work outside the home, or if one parent is moonlighting, the disadvantages often outweigh the advantages of more income.

Overworking creates stress and often requires hidden, unexpected expenses. What good is an extra $1,000 a month if you're constantly exhausted or if you rarely have time to spend with your children?

There is a growing movement in North America of couples and

Debt

THE BOTTOM LINE

"Debt is never the real problem. It is only symptomatic of the real problem: greed, self-indulgence, impatience, fear, poor self-image, lack of self-worth, lack of self-discipline, or something else."
—Ron Blue

families who are opting to live more simply. They're making the conscious choice to say "no!" to Madison Avenue. The results are that:

❀ Many are downsizing (either in the housing or in the automobile categories).

❀ Some are setting aside expensive hobbies and taking up other enjoyable, inexpensive pastimes—for example, enjoying fishing without having to buy a $20,000 boat. It's wisely been said that entertainment is expensive, but fun is cheap.

❀ Others are trading pricey vacations to tourist traps for less-expensive camping trips to state and national parks.

❀ Most are learning to shop less (staying out of the malls, trashing those mail-order catalogs, etc.).

❀ All are learning to shop smarter and to be creative.

Analyze and Adjust

Once you have a balanced budget in place, you can begin trying to live by it. And once you start living by it, you'll need to regularly analyze and adjust your financial plan. Put another way, the first three to four months of budgeting are highly experimental.

The biggest key in crafting an accurate budget is to keep careful records. It's wise to get in the habit of asking for and keeping sales receipts. Designate a central location (a drawer, a series of envelopes, a shoe box—some mutually agreed-upon place) in which to store all the paper you'll be collecting. For smaller cash purchases (soft drinks, newspapers, tips, etc.), you may wish to keep a little notepad in your pocket or purse in which you can write down everything that you spend.

"Do I Really Need to Write Down Everything?"

Initially, yes. Otherwise you may find that at the end of the month, you have $75 or more of unaccounted-for expenditures. Get in the receipt-keeping habit, and then every three or four days, take ten to fifteen minutes to record these expenditures in your budget book (available at any office supply store) or your financial computer program (see the final article in this section).

By carefully tracking *all* your expenditures, you will easily see where you need to adjust your new budget. Many first-time budgeters find that it is common to overestimate or underestimate what their expenses will be in certain categories. For example, you may find that, contrary to what you initially thought, you don't need to allocate $115 each month for "personal care" (i.e., toiletries, haircuts, etc.); in the first three months, you averaged only $80 a month in this category. Suddenly you have $35 "extra" to designate for something else. . .which is good, because upon further study you discover that your grocery bill (even when you have been comparison shopping and using coupons) is closer to $385 a month and not the $350 you had originally planned.

Do not fret. This kind of financial "give and take" is normal. Feel free to adjust your categories (making sure the total does not exceed your income). This is how wise families craft a workable budget. Keep tweaking your categories and numbers in this way, and after a few months you'll have a budget that really fits your lifestyle. Even though the process requires you to exercise fiscal discipline, it also will result—long-term—in robust fiscal health!

Remember also that though a budget is a wonderful guide and tool, it can't help you if you don't utilize it. Consult it regularly. Check your category totals often. For example, before you go grocery shopping, add up the totals in that category (or your saved receipts). If you've only got $54.67 left to spend this month, then don't spend more than that! Take a specific shopping list and a calculator. Stick to your guns. If you have no intention of living by a budget, it's really a waste of time to create one.

A "Set Aside Savings" Account

Some couples learn the hard way that even when they budget for quarterly, semiannual, or annual expenses (e.g., insurance premiums, tuition payments, dental visits, etc.), these "designated" monies are sometimes mysteriously missing from their checkbooks when the bills arrive. How does this happen? Consider the Thompsons' predicament. All last fall, they overspent in just a handful of categories (primarily, in "hobbies" and "clothing" and "groceries"). This doesn't sound like a major deal. However, when December rolled around, there was no expected surplus in their checking account for buying Christmas presents—even though, according to their budget, they should have accumulated $720 earmarked for holiday giving. Consequently, the Thompsons did what most families do. They whipped out their credit cards—and spent closer to

Financial Questions and Economic Deep Thoughts to Ponder:

- Why is the man who invests all your money called a *broker*?

- When someone asks you, "A penny for your thoughts," and you put your two cents in, what happens to the other penny?

- If 10 percent is good enough for God, shouldn't it be enough for the IRS?!

- Isn't the lottery really just a tax on people who are bad at math?

- Why do so many people spend their health for wealth, and then try to spend their wealth for health?

- Why do banks charge you a "nonsufficient funds fee" on money they already know you don't have?

$1,000. So much for a balanced budget!

What could the Thompsons have done instead? Many couples have discovered the wisdom of having a "set aside savings" account. Such a fund—ideally at the same bank where you have a checking account—gives you a safe place where you temporarily "hide" money you know you'll be needing in the months ahead. Imagine if the Thompsons had faithfully transferred $60 a month from their checking account into their "set aside savings" fund. By the end of the year, they would have been able to withdraw $720 in *cash* to spend on Christmas. The money would have been sitting there waiting for them. It would not have been spent on other items throughout the year. And they would not have succumbed to the credit trap.

You can take this same principle of setting aside money and use it to prepare for other future needs. In fact, it's possible to have assorted "hidden" savings accounts within your one "set aside savings" fund. Here at the lavish world headquarters of *The Indispensable Guides* (located just off Wall Street), we know of one family that uses this same system for numerous budget categories. Within a simple, regular bank savings account, they have monies set aside for Home (repairs & furnishings); Emergency Savings, Taxes, Insurance, Medical (including dental & prescriptions), Vacation, Clothing, Automobile (repairs), Education, and Christmas.

How does this plan work? At the end of each and every month, the couple faithfully transfers the total amount of these budgeted items from their checking account into their special "set aside" fund. They keep a notebook record of the exact amounts of money designated for each category. Later when bills arrive (e.g., a doctor's bill or a bill for plumbing work), they simply transfer that amount of money from their "set aside savings" account back into their checking and pay their debt. This wise plan guarantees that budgeted money will always be available for its planned purpose. When their $600 biannual car insurance premium arrives, the couple *never* panics about "Where are we going to find that money?" Why? They've budgeted and set aside $100 per month for the last six months in anticipation of this day. The bill arrives. They simply pay the premium and then reimburse their checking account (oftentimes, the same day by telephone) by transferring that exact amount from their "set aside savings."

This is a simple, painless, and ingenious way to keep out of trouble. Could such a "set aside savings" plan work for you?

Useful Computer Programs

Some people keep their financial records on scraps of paper in a cigar box. Others use an old-fashioned budget book (available for about $5 at an office supply store). There's really no "right" way. If a system works for you, use it. And if it ain't broke, don't fix it.

Another good way to make the budgeting process at your house a little more manageable is to utilize a personal finance software program on your PC or Macintosh.

One of the best and most popular applications today is Microsoft Money®, an easy-to-use program that can help you manage *all* your finances. Not only does Microsoft Money help you set up a budget and manage your check register, but it also keeps track of your income and expenses and all your accounts. In seconds, it can produce detailed graphs and reports about where all your money is going. In fact, if you want to know exactly how much money you've spent at the grocery store in the last forty-seven days, Microsoft Money can tell you in a matter of seconds!

It's also worth noting that at tax time, Microsoft Money works seamlessly with most major tax preparation software programs so that users are quickly and easily able to generate accurate and detailed forms for Uncle Sam.

The latest versions of this innovative financial tool give you the ability to create and maintain a home inventory, keep accurate records of all your investment portfolio, and track your net worth. In addition, by tapping into the power of the World Wide Web, Microsoft Money gives you all the help you need to make wise decisions about everything from mortgage rates to stock performances. Purchasing and utilizing a program like Microsoft Money is a very wise and very reasonable (usually about $50) investment.

Tithing

The Widow's Mite

If you went to Sunday school as a child you probably heard the story of the widow's mite. It's a short story listed in two Gospels, Luke and Mark. Here is Luke's account:

"As he looked up, Jesus saw the rich putting their gifts into the temple treasury. He also saw a poor widow put in two very small copper coins. 'I tell you the truth,' he said, 'this poor widow has put in more than all the others. All these people gave their gifts out of their wealth; but she out of her poverty put in all she had to live on' " (Luke 21:1–4).

This poverty-stricken widow is perhaps the most famous contributor to the local church. She has been lifted up from innumerable pulpits as an example, a beacon and. . .to be honest, sometimes a guilt stick to beat us into funding the ministries around us.

What do you think that poor woman was thinking as she approached the contribution bin? Why do you think she was willing to sacrificially give all she had to live on? Do you think her hands were shaking? Do you think her faith was strong? Do you think she wanted something from God? Do you think she gave out of loyalty to her synagogue? Do you think she was foolish to give all she had? Do you think God would rather have had her spend her money for groceries? Do you wonder if she even made enough income to have two pennies required as a tithe?

There are so many things we don't know about this woman, but these things we do know:

❀ She went to church.

❀ She gave even when it wasn't convenient.

❀ Her gift was seen by God.

And these are the things she teaches us:

She teaches us to support the church as the work of God in today's day and age.
God's Word teaches us that we are to give of our resources to the ministries of the church. In the Old Testament, the guidelines for giving were very specific. Church members gave a tenth of their money and crops. They gave their finest cattle and sheep. The teachings in the New Testament actually raise the bar in terms of tithing. The New Testament doesn't teach that there's a minimum we should give and then do what we want with the rest. The New Testament goes further than that and teaches us to give as people who feel the responsibility to minister to the world through the church.

She teaches us to give even when it isn't convenient and is even sacrificial.
The Bible teaches us that sacrificial giving is not a luxury we afford God; rather, it is the least we can do. We are to emulate God's sacrifice and find joy in giving of our resources so that God's work continues in our world.

She teaches us that our gifts, no matter how small, are seen by God.
God sees what we do in secret. Jesus made that clear in the Sermon on the Mount. God sees more than even the tax man or Uncle Sam does. God sees the nickels and dimes, the cash given when a check might have been more obvious. God sees our efforts and our sacrifice, no matter how small our gifts might seem in comparison to other people around us.

The widow who gave to her church, and thus to her God, all that she had to live on was the perfect picture of how God wants us to trust Him and thus to give to Him. You've probably already heard it many times, but we'll say it again, "We don't give to God because *He* needs us to; we give because *we* need to." We need to obey Him. We need to trust that He will provide. We need to do something out of love for a God who has done so much out of love for us.

The Tithe Threat

PERSPECTIVE

It seems like, at the first sound of disagreement in the church, someone is threatening to stop giving his tithe. There is an "I'll-hit-'em-where-it-hurts" mentality that causes us to run our mouths and shut our checkbooks when we often should do the opposite. Here is something to remember: You are a church member—not a customer. The church is not a vendor that you withhold payment from when it gives you bad service. You give to the church out of obedience to God. What your leadership does with that money has more to do with how you communicate with and trust that leadership, not whether you should obey God by tithing. If you take issue with the decisions being made regarding the direction of the church, your responsibility is to find a forum to voice your objections. This is not your cue to disobey God in order to teach someone a lesson or to express your power.

Do I Have To?

Sometimes it's difficult to tithe, to gift the church with a portion of your resources. Taxes take a big bite out of what you make in your salary and then to take even more out of your paycheck. . .well, sometimes it is an act of courage as well as of faith.

But the reality of the situation is that the resources that you have may *feel* like they belong to you, but there is a deeper reality. God has given you every bit that you have—whether it's money or kids or stuff, or the brains and will to earn the money and have the kids and buy the stuff. Everything that you have finds its source in God. He has called you to be manager of the resources that He has given you, just as surely as He gave the first man the responsibility to care for the garden.

PERSPECTIVE

A Picture of Tithing Written in Chocolate

If you want to get a good picture of God's view of tithing, think about the well-worn illustration of the box of candy. Imagine that you go to visit a child and take her a box of candy.

In one scenario the child thanks you for the gift and then opens the box and says, "Would you like the first piece?" That is a picture of biblical giving.

In another scenario, the child grabs the box, hides out in her room for a while, and then finally comes out to where you are sitting. With chocolate smeared all over her face, she offers you a piece of the candy that she didn't want. That is not a picture of godly giving.

The first scenario recognizes the source of the gift. When we tithe, that is exactly what we are doing: recognizing God as the source of the good things in our lives.

So do you *have* to give some of your resources back to God? Particularly your money (which is what seems to hurt the worst)? You do if you intend on living life according to God's guidelines. You do if you are committed to walking in faith the way God has asked you to. You have to trust God that much, that His plan works and that He will use the money you give back to Him. You have to believe that it matters to God that you contribute to His kingdom and that your resources will make a difference.

Will God break relationship with you if you don't? Will He not answer your prayers? Does God reject you when you don't give to His kingdom? God doesn't turn His back on His children when they don't obey Him, but His children sure do miss out on a lot when they walk away from God's plan. When you don't give to God's work, then you miss out on seeing God provide for you and for that work. That's a lot of joy tossed aside because you think you can't afford to obey.

Saving

A Cold Sweat

Bill leans across the table and stares you straight in the face. "Yep! And this year I'll have twice that in the bank. This sure is a good life I'm livin'. Yep. Sure is."

"Great, Bill!" You're trying to be enthusiastic for him, even though you're secretly envious of his success. "Got any hot tips for me?"

"Well. . . ," Bill nervously begins. You can tell he's trying not to say what he really thinks. "You know, this money thing is something you've got to figure out on your own. Besides, not everyone can do what I've done."

You mentally abuse yourself the whole way home. You're really not upset with Bill. In fact, you're really pleased with his success.

But what about yours? Why can't you achieve what he has?

You finally get home. Depressed, you slump into the easy chair and start channel surfing. Before long, you've drifted off.

You're awakened by the hospital. Your wife has been taken in for emergency surgery. She's unconscious—and they need your signature on the release form and a check for $3,000 to cover the insurance deductible. You're racing out the door when the phone rings again. It's your daughter's college. They haven't received this semester's tuition. They want a check for $5,000 mailed by the end of the week. You head to your car. . .sweating bullets. . .wishing this would all be over. You turn the key, and your car won't start.

You begin shaking your fists in the air. Frustrated. Angry. You never have enough to get by, and now everyone wants more. You begin to

Get a Better Handle on Your Concept of Saving Money

Finish this quick evaluation before you read any further.

I have a plan for saving.
Yes
No

I think saving is a good idea.
Yes
No

You've got to have a lot of money to begin saving.
Yes
No

It's better to save than invest.
Yes
No

Saving is a way to keep your extra cash available in case you need it.
Yes
No

A TRUCKLOAD OF CLUES

The Plan

Perhaps you're reading this section and you've tried saving, but it didn't work. Write out what your plan was and some of your ideas as to why the plan didn't work for you. If you'll do that now, you'll be able to apply the information more specifically as you read on.

_____

_____

Great! Now that you've written down your previous experience, read on through our ideas for what you can do to establish a healthy policy for saving.

cry when you hear your wife's soft familiar voice.

"Honey, what's wrong? Sweetheart? Wake up!"

A lot of people have the gift for putting money away. They've got a knack for saving their pennies and watching them grow into huge mounds of dollars.

Do you have that gift?

If you don't, we want this section to help you navigate through the "ins and outs" of saving. Here you'll find real help for beginning your savings plan, how to know what to spend your savings on, and how to find someone who can give you sound advice for your money.

So, wake up and let's get started.

Getting on top of the savings mountain isn't easy. You've got to think quick. You've got to work hard. And, most of all, you've got to have a plan.

There are four very distinct steps to beginning a successful savings plan. Take a moment and read these steps and consider if you've made any steps like these in the past. Get a better handle on your concept of saving money:

❀ Make a plan.

❀ Post your plan where your family can see it.

❀ Review the plan *before* you pay bills.

❀ Adjust the plan as needed.

Whether you've planned and carried out a savings plan before or if this is your first time, we think you'll find these four steps essential to your savings future.

Step One: Make a Plan

Making a plan for how you're going to save is the best, and the only proper, way to save. Now, before you throw up your hands and complain about how difficult making a savings plan is, take a moment to answer these questions. You might be surprised with the result.

Basically, your savings plan should include a list of things you dream of owning or obtaining and a list of things you need.

What do you dream of owning?

Want cash to buy a boat? Need some cash for a new fall wardrobe? Whatever you dream about, obtaining that dream is possible through a carefully thought-out savings plan.

Take a moment and write out some things you dream of owning. Try answering the questions for each saving objective you might have.

❀ I dream of owning. . .

_____

_____

❀ I dream of owning. . .

_____

_____

❀ I dream of owning. . .

_____

_____

So, now it's time for a little reality. Look back over these dreams of yours and ask yourself a few questions:

❀ Are these things I'm dreaming about attainable?

❀ Am I searching for something deeper?

❀ Will these things I'm dreaming about really satisfy me?

What are your needs?

It can be a difficult line to strike, but understanding the difference between your needs and wants is an important distinction when you're saving money.

THE BOTTOM LINE

Making a List, Checking It Twice. . .

Making the most out of these planning steps means that you'll need to prioritize your needs and wants. We suggest that you make two separate lists—one for needs and the other for wants. You can just write down some of the things you've already written down in this section. Then, prioritize those things on each list. Use some of the space below to accomplish that.

In the above section, we gave you a chance to write out some of your desires for the money you'll be saving. Now, we'd like you to think a bit more practically. Do you need to have some cash put aside to cover the deductible for your car, homeowner's insurance, or health insurance? How about some money put away for that extra, unexpected expense?

Take a moment and think through your needs. Consider the questions below and write out a few ideas.

❀ An immediate need (within the next six months) that I have is. . .

_____

_____

❀ A short-term need (within the next twelve months) that I have is. . .

_____

_____

❀ A long-term need (eighteen months and beyond) that I have is. . .

_____

_____

Now that you've written out a few of your financial needs, read through your ideas. Ask yourself these questions:

* Is everything I've written down a real need?

* Have I considered every need that might come up in my financial future?

* Have I written down a catchall account for unexpected expenses?

Step Two: Post the Plan

You've agonized over every detail of your savings plan. You've got a glimpse of where you might be with your savings in six, twelve, and eighteen months. Now for the easiest step you'll take in the process.

Posting the plan is simple. Put it everywhere you feel comfortable. If this is a significant event for you, you might even want to frame it and put it up in a place where everyone can see it. But don't just put it up and forget about it. Once you've put your savings plan everywhere you can think of, read through it daily. You might even want to discuss it over family meals now and then. Make it part of your weekly conversations with your spouse.

The key here is simple. The more you look at it, the more you'll talk about it. And the more you talk about it, the more you'll be conscious of what you're attempting to do. And you'll be more conscious of your spending if you've got a constant eye on your savings.

Now, here's where a little perspective is vital. It's important to keep a

Rhyme Time

A TRUCKLOAD OF CLUES

Okay, so you don't want to have to act real rational and seriously consider your savings plan every time you make a purchase? Consider making up a rhyme about your savings plan. That way, you won't feel like a drag reminding yourself about your commitment to save money.

Places You Might Want to Post Your Plan

PERSPECTIVE

Looking for safe places to put your savings plan? Try these:

* The refrigerator
* In your wallet—with your credit cards
* Your bathroom mirror
* In a safe place at your desk at work
* In the center of your kitchen table
* On the back of your television remote control
* In your car

constant eye on your savings plan, but keeping a constant watch on it might lead you to consider your savings more important than it really is. So, remember this: Watching your savings (and your spending) is important, but your money shouldn't become the focus of your life. If you *are* successful and are able to save a lot of money, remember that God gave you what you've saved, and you're just trying to do your best to manage it.

To help you keep your savings plan in perspective, we suggest praying through it with your family at least once a week. Whenever it's convenient for you, gather everyone together and spend time thanking God for His blessings. Then read through your plan, asking God to help you manage what He's given you. Ask for guidance in how you spend what He's helping you save.

Step Three: Review the Plan before You Spend
Does this describe you?

You're standing in line at the elevator, heading down to get your lunch out of the car. A coworker slaps you on the back, shakes your hand, and invites you to go with several people to a new medium-priced restaurant. Without batting an eye, you accept.

Or. . .

The bills have piled up, and you've got a free evening tonight. So, you decide to pay them. You begin at the top, working your way down until you're spent out.

Either of these come close to where you are? We're not saying that you

THE BOTTOM LINE

Cool, Calm, and Collected

Any smart savings plan ought to leave you calm. Comfortable. If you're stressing about your plan—either because you're not sure if you're correct in your number crunching, your goals, or your family's reaction to the idea—then your savings plan isn't really doing what it's designed to do.

It's important that you let the plan take over. That means, you ought to be able to sit back and enjoy the thought that you're saving money. So take some time and enjoy yourself. And, if you find you can't enjoy what's happening to your finances, it might be time to move to the next step.

should *never* go out with friends or that you shouldn't pay your bills. What we're suggesting is that in both of those situations, there's an essential step missing. Before heading out to do anything financial, whether it's paying bills or getting a little frivolous, it's essential to review your financial objectives—and that includes your savings plan.

For example, instead of sitting down to pay the bills and immediately writing checks, try looking over your savings sheet (it won't be too difficult if you've posted it all over your house, right?) and get your bearings. What are you saving for again? What are your financial objectives? If you can do this before you spend, you'll spend smarter. And you'll stick closer to the objectives you, and everyone else in your family, thought through rationally and clearly.

Step Four: Adjust the Plan As Needed

Any good plan might need some adjustments at first. And, as your needs change, your savings plan might just have to be adjusted. How do you adjust it?

❀ First, look at your spending habits since you've made your savings plan. Did you notice expenses that you might need to begin saving for? Did an expense creep up that you weren't expecting? If so, consider adding it to your list of things you're saving for.

❀ Next, look at the amount you are putting away. Is it putting a strain on your finances? Or, do you have more money left over at the end of the month? If so, adjust your plan accordingly.

❀ Finally, make small adjustments first. If you don't have enough money on hand, don't go crazy and quit saving altogether. Hold a little less back for savings and put the rest where you need it.

AMAZING STORIES
AND FACTS

For Money's Sake

"I know of nothing more despicable and pathetic than a man who devotes all the hours of the waking day to the making of money for money's sake."
—John D. Rockefeller (1839–1937), U.S. industrialist, philanthropist. Quoted in: Lewis H. Lapham, *Money and Class in America*, note to chapter 8 (1988).

Two Basics before You Begin. . .

As you're thinking about developing your plan, we want you to discover two very basic but essential elements of saving: when to start and how much you ought to be saving.

When should I start?

It's absolutely important that you begin saving as early as possible. If you've never saved before, it might feel weird to put money away and not plan on spending it. And that weird feeling might tempt you to delay a savings plan.

Consider this: Could you use an extra $600? You'd have that today if you had begun putting just $50 in a savings account twelve months ago. You'd have money to pay for that emergency trip to the mechanic, dentist, or doctor.

It's important to begin, but we recommend that you have a savings plan together before you begin saving. So, get that plan together and start working it. But don't wait for tomorrow. There are plenty of tomorrows left. And once the next one comes, you might be tempted to wait for the next one, and the next, and the next. . . .

How much should I save?

How much you save is very dependent on your savings plan. But in general, there are some tips you'll want to follow if you're just stashing money away for a rainy day.

❋ The 10 percent rule: If you're not sure how much to begin saving, try putting away 10 percent of your monthly earnings. It might help to take the amount you make yearly and multiply that by 10 percent. Divide that amount by 52 (the number of weeks in a year). Then, put that much away every paycheck.

For example, if you make $30,000 each year, you'd multiply that by 10 percent, which would be $3,000 each year. Then, divide $3,000 by 52 weeks, which would equal $57.70 each week. That's what you'd need to save each week in order to save $3,000, or 10 percent of your yearly income.

Don't feel strangled by our suggestion, though. You could up the ante and save more than 10 percent, or lower the percent you save until you get used to saving. The key is to get in the habit of putting money away for that important item or event you're planning for.

❋ Special gifts: If your family leans toward giving money as a gift instead of buying you something, consider slating that for savings. Or try saving a portion of every monetary gift you get.

Where to Park Your Cash

You've got cash. You're saving it and you need a place to put it. So, where do you put it?

Finding a good bank isn't that difficult. What should you look for? Well, *what* are you looking for? Take a moment and write down your ideal bank below. You can include anything you want from the architecture to the people who run the joint.

Now that you've got your dream bank down, look back over what you wrote.

❀ Were you concerned about the architecture? If you weren't, you *might* be a good candidate for someone who's interested in Internet banking. Especially if you're not even interested in ever entering your bank.

❀ Were you concerned about the people inside? You're definitely looking for a place where you'll feel comfortable with the people who handle your money.

❀ Were you concerned about the interest rate or availability of funds issues? You might want to consider a larger bank rather than a smaller one (larger banks are typically able to offer more services to their customers).

What All Banks Have

All banks offer the same basic services. Let's put those basic things on the table right now, just to get them out of the way.

All banks offer:

❀ savings accounts

❀ checking accounts

❀ some sort of CD program

❀ overdraft protection of some sort

❀ some sort of an automatic deposit of funds into your account (from your paycheck)

❀ automatic withdrawal from your checking or savings into a third-party account (for a bill or investment firm)

Now, here's where banks begin to get distinct and original. After offering these basic banking opportunities, banks morph themselves by offering more services that are aimed at gaining more customers, but they also hold some real advantages for you.

We've identified some of the additional options that many banks are making available. But be sure to check banks in your area to see if they offer these or other additional services that might make your banking easier.

Online banking
These days, a good bank is one that lets you have access to your account information via the Internet. All you need is your account number, a password, and Internet access.

Bill paying on demand
Along with the cool option of having Internet access to your account, you can create a pay-on-demand feature. If your account is accessible via the Internet, you might have the option of paying your bills online at your request.

Free checking
The banking industry has become very competitive. One of the neat features this competition has brought consumers is the option to have free checking accounts—often with no minimum balance.

Saturday banking
You might not need a bank that's open on Saturdays, but consider the advantages of banking with one that is. This can be especially helpful if you're out of cash but need to pay the piano teacher for that Saturday lesson.

Satellite locations
More and more, banks are moving into neighborhoods, making it easier for us to get to them. They're still full-service banks—just smaller and much easier to get to.

How to Park Your Cash
Parking your car the correct way is absolutely important. Park it the wrong way and you'll get a ticket, or your car might coast through the back wall of your garage. Parking your cash is the same way. But where exactly is the right place to put your money? As you're looking for the right way to park your cash, consider these options.

Hands-on accounts
If you're saving money for real-life emergencies (like emergency grocery money or cash to cover a possible checking overdraft), then you'll need to keep your money in a place where you can get your hands on it immediately. Some places you might want to consider would be:

* The family cookie jar. Okay, it doesn't have to be the cookie jar, but you might want to keep money on hand for emergencies. If you feel you need cash on hand, remember that holding on to your money this way is a sure way to spend it quickly. So, if you're planning on keeping cold, hard cash on hand, be sure that you've got the self-control not to spend it.

* A bank account. These days, you can tie your savings in with your checking. And, if you've got a bank that provides Internet banking, you've got instant money when you need it.

Hands-off accounts

If you're putting money away for college for your kids, for a car, or possibly insurance deductibles, you might want to drift toward a hands-off account.

Hands-off accounts are exactly what they sound like. They're savings accounts that you use to store money in, but you *never* touch that money—no matter what.

Finding a place you can put your money and never touch it isn't that easy. Most of what you might face is your ability to keep your hands off the money you've saved. However, you might want to try these options:

* Open a savings account and forget you've got it. Once you've set up the account, ask the bank to withdraw money from your checking account into your savings. Then, forget about that money. Imagine you don't have it. Hide your savings book so you'll never really know the account number. That way, when you *think* you need the money, you won't touch this private account.

* Put your money away in a difficult-to-access location. Many banks offer money market accounts. Consider opening one in another state (easy to do through the Internet).

Breaking the Bank

You've been really, really good. The plan you created to help yourself save money is really working. You feel comfortable. Then, one day, you're at the mall with your friend. Those shoes you've had your eyes on are finally on sale. However, they're still really expensive—even with the sale. You're close to the end of your money in your checking account. Is this something you spend some of your savings on?

That depends.

Knowing when to spend the money you've saved is an intensely personal subject. We can't make the decision for you. However, we do want to give you some general ideas for when you might want to consider breaking your piggy bank.

Before you spend it. . .
Ask yourself these questions when you're tempted to spend from your savings.

❀ *Does this expense fit with why I'm saving?*
If you're saving money to pay off a medical expense, a new pair of shoes doesn't fit with your plan.

❀ *How will I feel after I buy this item?*
Try and imagine yourself three days after you've purchased the item. Will it really help you? Will you really be happier or more content?

❀ *Do I really need this item?*
Impulse purchases can really make a huge dent in your savings account. Before you buy, be sure that you really need the item. You might want to walk away from purchasing it immediately and take some time to think about it. Remember—what you want to buy will probably be there later.

A Financial Friend

Do any of these categories fit you?

❀ You're a millionaire and you're not sure where to put your cash. Stocks? CDs? Overseas investments?

❀ You're a husband of a family who makes just enough to survive. You're feeling the need to store away some "just in case" money.

❀ You're an average person. You're financially comfortable. But you're convinced you could do more with the excess that God has provided.

Whether you're a financial guru or you just need someone to bounce your money ideas off of, you just might need a financial advisor.

Buy why? What does a financial advisor offer you that a trusted neighbor might not?

They Know the Market
If your job is to groom iguanas, you probably know the ins and outs of iguanas: what they eat, how they eat, why they always look so unhappy, etc. The same goes with financial advisors. It's their business to know the stock market and interest rates. But it's also their job to know a lot more.

Financial advisors also have to know nearly every financial institution out there. That way, they'll know the best place for you to park your money.

They Have Resources at Their Fingertips

Because of who they are and whom they might know, financial advisors have a lot of resources at their fingertips: info on financial institutions, special money-planning software, insight into the best money maneuvers ever thought up. It might be difficult for us to know the heart of a bank president. Many financial advisors might know that info.

They Can Offer Objective Advice

Financial advisors make money by giving you advice, moving paperwork around, and helping you make smart financial decisions (their rates differ depending on the type of advice, level of involvement in your financial affairs, etc.). But still, these people can look at your financial situation and give you solid, objective advice about what you ought to do with your cash.

Shopping for a Financial Advisor

Convinced that you need someone to advise you about your money? Go shopping for a moment and choose from one of these qualified people.

Frieda

She's got ten years in the banking industry, most of which was spent as a teller. Recently she's gained a lot of experience in the inner workings of the banking industry as a loan officer. Frieda isn't always on time, but she's always honest with you about her opinions regarding your money. She also works as a night cashier at the Gas-N-Sip on the weekends.

William

You've seen his picture on the wall of your bank since before you can remember. Last year, you became friends with William when you met him at a charity function. William knows finances better than anyone you've met. He's proud. Stodgy. Almost prudish. Like Frieda, William is very opinionated, but every financial advice paragraph he speaks begins with the words, "Well, if you've really got the money you say you do. . . ," leaving you to think your relationship might be more prince versus pauper. And you ain't no prince.

Ken

Ken's been your best buddy since high school. In fact, you were on the soccer team together. You kept in contact with Ken all through college. Now that the two of you are back in the same town together, you've grown closer than before. Ken's occupation is (guess what!) financial planning. He's no expert, but you trust him.

Those three descriptions are similar to what you'll find as you begin your search for a trusted financial advisor. Real people. People who are normal, abnormal, and everything in between. How can you refine your search and know what type of person you're looking for?

It begins with your expectations. You've got to know what you're looking for before you go shopping. So, start from scratch here. Write out a few of your expectations, and then we'll give you some places to refine your search.

I expect the following qualities in my financial advisor:

_____

_____

What Qualities Should You Be Looking For?

❀ *Someone you like*

First and foremost, find someone you like. You're about to search for someone who will advise you about a very important issue in your life. You might even be trusting this person to handle your financial affairs. You want someone you like. Someone you feel comfortable being around.

❀ *Someone you trust*

You probably know the moment you meet someone if you would trust him with your money. It's an inner feeling that you have—or don't have.

❀ *Someone who doesn't drive a Ferrari*

Okay, this might not seem like that big of a deal to you. But have you ever thought that someone you're trusting your money to, who drives a really expensive car or lives very well, might just have had to earn that money? And, if they're earning it from you, then are you being charged too much? Just remember this rule of thumb—if your potential financial advisor lives much better than you do, he or she might not be the best person to handle your finances. Yet you also want to know that the person is. . .

❀ *Someone who has demonstrated financial success*

You wouldn't give a baby a paintbrush and get upset when she didn't paint your portrait perfectly, right? The same goes for someone you're entrusting with your money. You want to look for someone who has demonstrated financial success in his or her personal finances and someone who's been successful managing the finances of others.

❀ Someone who's godly

This is a tricky one because it might not be the easiest subject to broach with a potential financial advisor. Begin by asking if he goes to church. Then go further with the conversation if you feel you need to. Basically, look for someone with whom you feel compatible in this area. It's important that the two of you share basic beliefs about spiritual issues. Will he understand your desire to tithe or give money to missions? Will he stare blankly at you when you mention the financial gifts God has given you?

How to Find the Right Advisor

Hitting the bricks and finding someone who can advise you about your finances doesn't have to be a drain on your emotions and spirit. What's the best way to search out your trusted financial advisor?

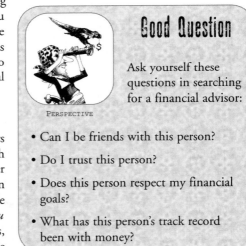

PERSPECTIVE

Good Question

Ask yourself these questions in searching for a financial advisor:

- Can I be friends with this person?
- Do I trust this person?
- Does this person respect my financial goals?
- What has this person's track record been with money?

❀ Interview people.

Interviewing potential advisors is as simple as eating lunch with them, inviting them over for dinner, or visiting them in their office. Ask them simple questions about things *you* understand about finances, and see if their answers jibe with what you know. Be sure to ask personal questions, too: marriage, children, and goals for life.

❀ Ask your friends.

If your friends have had any dealings with financial advisors, now's the time to ask them. Ask everyone. Who? Your pastor just might be the best person to begin asking. He probably knows a lot of financial people in your community. And, remember this: With the offerings, gifts, and other financial hoops your church jumps through every year, he probably has at least one financial advisor whispering various ideas in his ears.

❀ Ask for references.

It's perfectly okay to ask your prospective financial advisors to provide you with names and phone numbers of people they've helped with their finances. If a potential advisor balks at your request, take that as a subtle sign that he might not be the person you're looking for. Once you've got some names, take time to call a few of the people. Introduce yourself and explain that you're considering using this person as your financial advisor. Explain that you got their name from your potential advisor, and ask them for their feelings about the person.

❀ *Ask about their personal finances.*

Another area that might be touchy, but it's vitally important that you get a sense of what your potential candidates do with their personal finances. You don't have to get specific details about their finances, but you do need to ask some pointed questions about how they've handled their money.

To get a picture of their financial position, consider asking these questions:

❀ What percentage of your money do you save every month?

❀ When did you begin saving money?

❀ What are some of your future financial goals?

❀ *Ask to see their offices.*

We really aren't being picky with this one, but it goes to the heart of basic rules of organization. You might want to look for someone whose office has a reasonable sense of order. You want someone who can organize himself properly. You'll be allowing this person to help you manage your hard-earned money—you'll need him to be organized. Having your papers in proper order (minus the mustard stains) and remembering your upcoming meeting are qualities that you need in a strong candidate for a financial advisor.

To get a picture of their offices, you might want to consider having your initial meeting with them in their office. Look for organizational clues like file cabinets, Rolodexes, a calendar close by, etc.

Investing

The Journey Begins. . .

You've been watching the news, surfing the Web, asking friends for weeks. Finally, the moment has arrived. After dumping most of your savings into a hot stock a friend suggested, you wait patiently.

Day one:

The stock does nothing. It ends the day at the same price that it began the day. Sigh. You expected this. But you hoped for a more exciting day.

Day two:

The market was volatile today. Huge tech stocks weighed the market in the morning, driving it significantly lower in the morning session. Then, late in the day, there's a sudden surge. The market races toward a new high. You're proudly riding that wave with a fifteen-dollar increase in your stock. You go out for dinner that night. You can afford it.

Day three:

You wish today had never begun. "Maybe I'm too into this stock market thing," you say to yourself. Your stock takes a real beating. Analysts promise that tomorrow will be a much better day.

THE BOTTOM LINE

A Word about Your Strategy

Now that you've asked yourself important questions about savings, you can get a clearer picture of how you're going to attack the market. Depending on your goals, you'll want to consider these timelines.

Short Term: If you're just wanting to put some cash in the market and work it for two years until a family vacation, you'll want to consider yourself a short-term investor. Buying on the short-term timeline means that you might want to get involved in more volatile stocks. The risk is great, but the returns can be higher over the short term.

Long Term: If you're in the market for a longer period of time and you don't want to take your money out anytime soon, consider looking at stocks that are steady growers and well-established companies. These stocks aren't as exciting as fast-moving stocks but generally outperform over the long haul.

Day four:

Today was supposed to be a better day. . .probably was for other people. Not for you, though. Your stock hits a new all-time low. The news is out, too—the CEO of the company quits, and earnings are well below expectations. Your stock is in trouble. You decide to bail tomorrow.

Day five:
You wake up in a cold sweat. You rush to the TV. Everyone's talking about the stock you've been sweating about all week. Things are looking up. The price isn't the same as when you bought in, but it's looking better. You take some aspirin and ride out the day. Things look like they'll be okay.

Investing in the market. It's not easy. It's not for everyone. But it might just be for you. We want this chapter to help you understand the market. If you're planning on investing, this chapter will help you get a very basic understanding of how the market works and how you can get started in it.

What to Remember about the Market
Before you begin investing, there are basic things everyone should know about the stock market. Most of this you might already know, but it's essential information for proper stock picking and a good investment strategy.

Must Do

A TRUCKLOAD OF CLUES

Three initial "must do's" might sound intimidating, but they're really not. How can you get some knowledge and still have a life?

- Begin surfing now. We've put a list of web pages in the "Resources for Further Enlightenment" section that you'll want to look at as you begin understanding more about the market.

- Hit the library. There's a ton of books available. You might just want to scan some magazines. We've put some of those in the "Resources for Further Enlightenment" section.

- Watch and listen. News on the radio and television offers stock market updates. Take some time and check out what they're saying about the market and the economy.

Driven by the economy

The stock market moves with the economy. So, if buying clothes is up and you own shares of a popular clothing company, you just might profit from your careful decision. However, if you own shares of an automotive maker and they're really getting hit this year, you're probably going to suffer.

That can help you somewhat. Knowing that the market is driven by the economy means that there are times you can predict that some "sectors" of the economy will do well: toy companies during Christmas, resorts during the summer months.

So, the first step in investing is to know the economy. As your interest in the market begins to take shape, try reading magazines that research the economy or different parts of it. And you might want to surf Web pages that deal with what parts of the economy are expected to do well for the upcoming quarter. Get to know the economy, what fuels it, and what businesses are good at different times of the year.

Driven by someone's word

It's no secret what happens on Wall Street. Someone talks. Maybe a television anchor. Maybe a respected economist speaking about the economy. Whoever it is, if they're important and they've got an opinion (and one that people will listen to), the financial world can climb or dive based on their comments.

Welcome to the emotional side of the market. Many people who crunch numbers all day deal only with the hard truths of the market. What will a certain company's earnings be this year? Will the latest Internet stock make its quota this quarter? But the emotional side of the market seeks out advice, opinions, and savvy community-based research that will give information about what's happening in the market and in the economy. A simple suggestion that a major Internet provider might not make its earnings estimates can send the stock plummeting, even when no one has spoken from the company about their earnings at all.

So, as you're beginning your study in investing, remember these two very important factors. The nonemotional side of the market involves knowing the economy. Getting to know how things work in the market—you've got to know that. But the other side—the emotional side—is important to master, as well. Know the people to whom everyone in the market listens. Get a feel for what comments make companies (and investors) happy, and what comments cause people to run for the hills (and sell their stock and drive the market down). Mastering these two sides of the market is important as you begin your investment trek.

Moves very fast

One last thing we want you to know. The stock market moves at a lightning pace. Here are truths about the market that you'll need to grasp before you begin investing.

❀ Stocks rise and fall second by second. That means that buying a stock at a certain price that you're comfortable with means you sometimes have to move quickly.

❀ What's hot one day isn't necessarily hot the next. If a certain stock rose sharply today, and you're thinking about buying it tomorrow, it won't necessarily rise again tomorrow.

❀ Getting a grasp of this lightning-speed pace will mean that you'll need to know a lot about the market so you'll be able to do a little predicting. In other words, if you understand what drives the market up and whom to listen to (both of the above comments), then you'll need to put that knowledge to the test and predict along with the others.

Steps to Investing

You've decided that you've got what it takes to invest in the market. You're not scared. . .in fact, you're welcoming the challenge. So, how do you get started?

There are a lot of different ways you can get yourself connected to the stock market and numerous other ways you can begin trading. However, we'd like to suggest a simple outline you might follow. *If* you know a lot about the market, you might consider writing your own plan of attack. However, if you feel you need a little guidance, feel free to follow some of our ideas.

1. Pick Your Sector

What in the world is a "stock sector" anyway? Simply put, it's a group of companies that make up a particular grouping of industries. Some examples of stock sectors include the Tech Sector, the Transport Sector, and the Retail Sector. And, as you might guess, different companies belong to the appropriate sector. For example, a company making clothes would belong to the Retail Sector. An airline company would belong to the Transport Sector.

Picking your sector before choosing your stocks is vital. Many people know one sector better than another. So, ask yourself, *What sector do I know the most about?* Need help? Check out the following page. Circle the top three sectors that you feel you know the best.

2. Pick Your Method

Deciding how you'll invest can be as tricky as deciding what you'll buy. You've got two options open to you as you step out to pick a method of investing.

IMPORTANT REMINDERS

Need Some Help?

Here's a list of the Standard and Poor's nine stock sectors with examples of the types of businesses in each.

Financial—Life insurance companies and major regional banks

Staples—Food, beverage, and prescription drug companies

Technology—Computer software and hardware, chip manufacturers, long-distance phone companies

Services—Hotels, media, tax preparation companies

Industrial—Glassmakers, construction, and manufacturing equipment companies

Utilities—Natural gas and electric companies

Basic Industry—Aluminum, chemicals, mining, and paper products companies

Cyclicals—Transportation industries such as railroads and airlines; consumer cyclical industries such as appliance manufacturers, clothing companies, toymakers

Energy—Petroleum refining, electrical power plant construction, petroleum and gas exploration industries

Going on your own. . .

The Internet has brought with it the option of investing on your own. Long ago (about five years) you had to go through a broker to invest your money. However, these days, investing has become as simple as wiring some money into an online investing account.

Investing on your own is an adventure if you like being in charge of your own money. If you're planning on heading out into the investment world on your own, remember these important facts.

❀ Going it alone means just that. Without an investment broker, you won't have the help of an experienced investor helping you make decisions.

❀ If you're not using a broker, you'll have to do your own trading. So, if you're planning on selling a stock when it hits the price you're looking for, how will you accomplish that?

Using a broker

Using a broker is a tried-and-true method. And if you're a new investor and have enough money to pay a broker's commission, you might want to consider using a broker at first (by the way, if you're looking for a broker, we've put those at the end of the book in our "Resources for Further Enlightenment" section).

If you're planning on using a broker, keep these things in mind.

A TRUCKLOAD OF CLUES

Looking for an Online Investment Company?

There are many to choose from. More are added to the Internet all the time. Even large brokerage firms are establishing themselves online. How can you find one that's right for you?

- Know the difference between discount and full-price brokers. Discount brokers don't offer much advice (if any), but you can trade stocks for a nominal transaction fee. Full-price firms offer advice and more options for more money.

- Review several online brokers and find one you like. They're all different.

- Check out their initial investment policy. How much cash do they require to open your account?

- Find out what research they offer for free and what research you have to pay for.

※ Commissions vary depending on the broker. Some are around $20, some higher, others lower. You pay these commissions each time you buy or sell stock.

※ Using a broker means that you'll be adding another person into your investment ideas. They'll be involved in your strategy. Are you comfortable with that?

※ Brokers handle a lot of people at one time. They might not be able to give you personalized service all of the time, and they might not be accessible to you every time you need them.

3. Pick Your Stock

It's that time. Time to decide what stock you want to purchase. So, how do you know what stock is right for you?

What do you like?

Earlier, we asked you to pick your favorite sector. Now, it's time to pick your favorite stock, or a few stocks in the sectors you like most. Once you've picked these stocks, begin watching them.

What to pick?

Hmm. Good one. Ask yourself these questions:

❀ What companies am I interested in?

❀ What companies do I hear others talking about?

❀ What stocks do I think might rise in the next few months/years/decades?

THE BOTTOM LINE

What's an Upgrade?

We're not talking about something new you can add to your computer. Upgrade/downgrade lists are available many places online, through a brokerage house, or through your online investment company.

An upgrade/downgrade listing contains a list of stocks that major investment firms are recommending as buys, encouraging their clients to sell, or sometimes recommending that people hold. They're often looked at as one source for seeing how stocks might do in the coming weeks.

What's recommended?

It's important to begin checking around for stocks that are being recommended: Which news service is looking at what stocks? Who's bragging about their earnings beating the expectations of various analysts? What stocks are listed on different "upgrade/downgrade" lists?

AMAZING STORIES AND FACTS

Peculiarly Dangerous

"October. This is one of the peculiarly dangerous months to speculate in stocks in. The others are July, January, September, April, November, May, March, June, December, August, and February."
—Mark Twain (1835–1910), U.S. author. *Pudd'nhead Wilson*, chapter 13, "Pudd'nhead Wilson's Calendar" (1894).

If you're going it alone, try searching through various Web sites, magazines, and newspapers for stocks in your sector that others are talking about. If you're not alone in this venture (meaning you've coupled with others who know what they're doing, or you're using a broker), then bounce a few ideas off of them, or ask them what their suggestions might be.

In short, we're encouraging you to do as much research as you can. If you're not in a hurry to buy, consider opening your investment account and letting it accumulate simple interest while you research your final stock selections. If you're not sure where to begin researching, we've placed some ideas for you in the section titled, "Resources for Further Enlightenment."

Dollar Cost Averaging

PERSPECTIVE

Investing a set amount in the market or in mutual funds is called "Dollar Cost Averaging." Simply put, when you invest the same amount every month, you're buying stocks or funds at their highs and at their lows. When you figure the average price you're buying at, it usually works out that you're buying stock much cheaper than putting one lump sum in.

4. Pick Your Target

This step isn't really a major one since there's not much you can do to change the price of a stock. However, there are some important things for you to consider here.

If you've picked your stock by now, you probably know what price it's trading at. And, if you've done some research, you know what the stock has traded at in the past, and what analysts are saying about its future. All of that should give you a good indication of the future price of the stock. At this point, you need to decide if the stock is something that you can afford and if that stock will go up in its price over the time you've decided to stay invested in it.

Begin asking yourself these questions:

❀ Is this stock at a price that I think I can afford?

❀ Do I think that the price of this stock will go significantly higher?

❀ What price might I want to sell the stock at, if it does go higher?

Target picking is important. Often investors will rush into a hot stock, buy it, and hunker down and wait for whatever financial crisis (but hope there isn't one) that might come along. These people haven't picked a target; they've picked a stock and drawn a target around it. This approach is risky. You can lose money more often with this approach. It's best to pick first, then buy.

When Should I Begin Investing?

Now. You should begin investing now.

Why? Because time is your friend—the earlier you invest, the longer your money has a chance to grow. And, though the stock market has had many rocky moments over the years, the general trend of stocks is upward.

If you're really fortunate, you could catch the market on an upswing. Consider that a $1,000 investment in America Online in the early 1990s was worth over $600,000 by the end of the decade. Many such "success stories" appear in the annals of investing.

Of course, we're not sug-

THE BOTTOM LINE

You've Got the Time

One important tip to remember when investing in the stock market is that time is on your side. The longer you hold on to a good stock, the more money you stand to make. For example, The Motley Fool (a Web site available to you with a lot of great free advice) notes that if you had put $1 in the stock market in the year 1900, you'd have over $10,000 today. You can make money in the stock market, but as with most good financial growth, it takes time.

gesting that you'll make that much money that quickly every time. The point is that the sooner you begin investing, the sooner your money can work for you.

One other thing you ought to be aware of: Buying stocks sooner rather than later is important. But so is buying stocks often. It can be easy to put some money in the market, and then step back, watch your stock, and wait. But there's another way. Consider putting money into the market regularly. Set up a plan for investing in the market every month or every week by asking your brokerage firm if they will automatically deduct an amount you instruct as often as you request.

How Much Should I Invest?

The question of how much to invest is a looming one. The actual decision about how much you should invest at first and then over the course of your interest in investing depends on *how* you plan on investing.

To trade stocks, you'll need a lump sum to open your investment account. Some discount online brokerage firms allow you to open your account with an initial investment of $1,000. Other brokerage firms require that you have $5,000 to $10,000 to open your account. These funds go into a money market account and you can trade from that. Remember: You don't *have* to invest all of that money in the market if you don't want to. Consider buying just a few shares of one or two stocks to get started. Then increase your shares or your trading activity as you feel more comfortable.

If you're investing in mutual funds, the initial amount you have to invest gets lower. Many mutual fund companies allow you to begin investing in their mutual funds with an initial investment of $50 or less. If you're buying CDs, you'll usually need at least $500 to get started.

Besides the initial investment, you'll want to consider one question as you set out to invest. How much are you willing to lose? We don't want to be negative, but the truth is, the market comes with its ups and downs. While it's highly unlikely that you'll lose *everything* if your stocks go south, you might lose a significant amount as in the recent bear market. If you've never invested before, and you've chosen to invest on your own, you might want to consider investing a little bit at first. Make a few trades, get a feel for how the system works, and check out your ability to predict how stocks move.

Weighing the Differences: Stocks, Bonds, and Funds

Imagine this:

You've just entered a huge cookie store. This is a big deal for you because you *love* cookies. You're ready to dive in. You reach for your money—not there. "Ahh, that's right. I put it in my front pocket," you say to yourself. So you plunge your hand into your pocket with wild anticipation. No money. Now you remember. You left it on your dresser.

So, you begin to slump out of the store when you see the sign TODAY ONLY. FREE COOKIES FROM 2:00–4:00. It's 2:30, and you're ready to party.

You go wild. Chocolate with almonds. Peanut butter delights. Sugar-topped with strawberries. After about thirty minutes, you roll out, waving a sticky-handed good-bye to your new favorite friend—the owner.

What could be better than this?

Investing. (Okay, stop laughing.)

When you open an investment account, you're not bound to one type of investment. Rather, you've just entered a huge financial world where you can put your money virtually anywhere—anywhere in the world, in any company, and at any frequency you choose. It's like walking into a cookie store! You're welcome (though not for free) to help yourself to a seemingly infinite number of companies that grow, change, and innovate.

We want to introduce you to three main investment opportunities (nope, we're not talking about some swampland we're trying to unload). There are a lot of different investments out there. While most fall under these three areas, there are others. These three, however, are the ones most often chosen by investors.

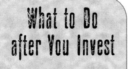

What to Do after You Invest

• *Watch it.*
A TRUCKLOAD OF CLUES It's important to keep an eye on your money. However, it's also very important not to go crazy about watching it. Maybe set aside a certain part of your day that's okay for you to turn on the television or surf over to a Web page and check on your stock.

• *Forget about it.*
It's okay to keep your eye on your stock. But it's also okay to forget about it once you've begun—especially if you're planning on holding on to a stock for a long period of time.

• *Continue to research.*
While you're watching your stock (or not watching it), you might want to continue to research it now and then. Keep abreast of news that affects your stock by devoting about an hour or two a month to reading up on various things that affect your stock.

Stocks

If you're a company who needs operating capital, one way for you to raise that money is to jump through hoops, get yourself approved for a public offering on the stock market, and hope people buy your stock. In turn, for people giving you money, you give investors stock in your company. They have a vote in what you do, and you have more cash to operate your business.

Stocks vary in price from penny stocks (less than $5.00 per share) to some well into the hundreds of dollars per share. You buy stocks through a brokerage firm who charges you for the transaction. Companies often list millions of their shares on the major stock exchanges.

We've said it a lot already in this chapter, but it's something worth repeating. Stocks are probably the most volatile way to invest.

When they go up, they offer great returns on your money. But if they don't go up in price, you might not be a happy camper.

Buying stocks is simple. You buy a stock when it's priced low, then you hold on to it until its price rises. Fairly simple, right?

Mutual Funds

While stocks could be highlighted as a risky type of investment, mutual funds highlight themselves as creatively removing much of that risk by buying a lot of stocks and combining them into funds and hiring a fund manager to look after it.

Mutual funds are simple to understand, and they're a little easier on the nerves. When you buy a mutual fund, you're actually buying a lot of stocks all at once. The fund price goes up and (just as in stocks) you've made some money. Mutual funds are less risky because if one of the stocks in the fund is down, another might be up. And, if all of the stocks in a fund take a hit, the impact on your shares might be less severe.

Bonds

Bonds are very different from both stocks and mutual funds. They're the equivalent of you loaning the government cash so it can operate. Hey, even the government needs a loan to operate every now and then. And they get it from you.

Bonds are typically sold in $1,000 increments. You're paid a fee for giving the government money to work with. Bonds are less risky to invest in because you can usually trust the government to repay its debts. We say *usually* because there are investors out there that don't buy bonds because they feel they're *more* risky than stocks.

Whatever investment you choose, we wish you all the success in the world. It's no fun putting your money into something and then losing part of that investment. So here's hoping that you're successful and pleased with your stock choices, strategy, and the return on your choices.

Children

Teaching Children About Money

Rather than beat around the bush, we're going to start this chapter out being very blunt: It is imperative that you teach your children about money. If you want your children to handle money successfully, you have to teach them how. If your children are young enough not to have picked up any bad money habits, you still have the chance to start out on the right foot. But if you have children who constantly pester you for money or have no concept of its value, it's time to make some changes. Fortunately, habits can be changed and money dilemmas solved. Although the solution will vary from family to family, there are some basic ground rules for teaching children about money.

Money Skills to Be Learned

As parents, you must take deliberate steps to teach your children specific skills if they are to handle their money responsibly both now and when they get older. Even if you feel like your upbringing in this area was poor, you can help your children start out on the right foot by teaching these money skills.

Spending money wisely

The first thing children learn to do with money is spend it. It takes no time at all for them to learn how to exchange a quarter for some candy. But teaching them how to spend it *wisely* is the key. First, place limits on how much you give them. Even if you're someone with a disposable income or you feel guilty about the divorce, do your children this favor. It helps them understand that money has value and its supply is not endless. Second, give advice on how to spend smart. While the example you set for your children is highly important, don't assume that they will pick up wise spending habits just through observation. Make them aware of prices. Teach them about coupons, discounts, when sales usually are; that the same item may cost more or less in another store; and not to purchase on a whim.

PERSPECTIVE

Saving for Something Special

"When I turned twelve, I really wanted a ten-speed bike like my best friend, but it was way more expensive than anything I had ever saved money for. So my dad sat down with me and showed me how to budget my money so I could save enough to get the bike. It was such a great feeling to go in the bike shop and have enough money to pay for the bike myself!"

—Shawn, Durango, Colorado

Budgeting

If your children have jobs or some source of income, it's time to teach them a simple budgeting system. You could start by showing them your household budget. Not only will this give them a good idea about budgets, it will show them how important it is to plan and know where each dollar is going. Let them create their own budget. It's especially helpful if they have a goal of purchasing something. Having a budget will help them keep track of their expenditures and plan how to save to reach their goal.

Saving

That old saying "You can't teach an old dog new tricks" isn't really true. It's just harder. The same is true with kids and money. The older they get, the harder it is for them to learn to save because they've gotten used to buying what they want now. The key is to start teaching children as young as possible how to save. Again, don't fret if your children are in high school. Just start by identifying something they really want, something you might normally buy them, and explain they will have to save and buy it themselves. But then don't just turn and walk away. Go back with them to their budget and show them how to save and how long it will take. Keep it relatively inexpensive for the younger child, but the junior higher is mature enough to go without today to get something later.

Borrowing

We write a check here, swipe the credit card there, and barely give a thought to credit. It's simply a way of life these days. But kids need to know that magical card is not free money. Give them practical experience in borrowing so they come to understand if they borrow today, the money must be paid back at a later date. Sit down with them and show them on paper or with real money that if they make $2.00 this week and borrow $1.75, they will have $3.75 to spend, but next week they will only have 25¢ left over after they pay back the $1.75. Another hint? Don't let them start a borrowing pattern from siblings or future allowances. They need to learn that there won't always be someone to bail them out in the future.

Tithing

Even though we've included it at the bottom of the list, tithing should be one of the first things children learn about their money. If you personally tithe and give an allowance, it might seem silly to expect your children to tithe in addition, but don't neglect to give them the opportunity to show their appreciation to God for His gifts. Even a young child can put money in an envelope and drop it in the offering plate at church or mail it to a favorite ministry or charity. Be sure it's clear that the money is not going back into your pocket, and show older children how to include tithing in their budget.

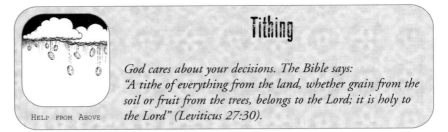

God cares about your decisions. The Bible says:
"A tithe of everything from the land, whether grain from the soil or fruit from the trees, belongs to the Lord; it is holy to

HELP FROM ABOVE   *the Lord" (Leviticus 27:30).*

When and How to Teach Your Children about Money

Don't fool yourself into thinking your children will just pick up how to handle money from watching you or your spouse spend it. And we recommend not waiting until your children are old enough to start begging for money to consider teaching them. It doesn't take long for the constant barrage of "Mommy, I want that r–e–a–l–l–y bad," or "I need money for this; I need money for that" to get on your nerves. So come up with a game plan to help your children learn to handle money responsibly. Your plan will depend on the ages of your children and what they can understand. Since the odds are that you're not a child psychologist, we've broken down the ages and what you should be teaching to guide your plan.

Birth to three years old

At this age, just keep track of when the last diaper was changed and skip the lessons with real money. You don't want to make a run to the emergency room because Junior stuck the penny in his nose while you went to answer the phone.

Four to six years of age

Preschool children can make decisions for themselves, as you may well know from the overly used phrase "I do it myself." But since they can't think logically yet, keep your teaching simple. Start with basic introductions to bills and coins. After explaining their value and purpose, let your children experience using money. Here's an example of one mother's method of developing her son's decision-making skills while introducing him to money:

> "Before we go to the store, I give Mark fifty cents to spend on anything in the store he wants. I always make it clear that fifty cents is the limit. The first time he chose candy that cost fifty-five cents, but I didn't give him another nickel, *even* after he threw a tantrum. He had to choose something else that he could buy with fifty cents or less. Now he gets so excited to go to the store and purchase something. He is very thoughtful about what he wants and is learning about prices."
>
> —Carol, Claremont, New Hampshire

Don't waste your time trying to teach young children about saving money. Since they have no concept of the future, they don't connect putting coins in a piggy bank with what they can do with the money later. Money to them is something to be used now and is always available when needed. (Wouldn't it be nice if that were true for the rest of us?!)

Seven to twelve years of age

Children in this stage are able to think more logically and systematically, but they still have their limitations. When explaining money, be as concrete as possible. Count with real money and do simple arithmetic to get your point across. Teach them how to make change. Give them opportunities to pay for the movie or ice cream or when you get gas. Here's an example of one father's way of teaching his child that the things they do cost money:

A TRUCKLOAD OF CLUES

Rule of Thumb

Young children can learn about money. But trying to teach too much information too soon will only frustrate both you and your child.

> "One evening our family went out to dinner, and I taught my eight-year-old son how to pay the bill and decide how much to tip the waitress. He got a real kick out of it and now likes to pay for whatever we do. Rather than using my credit card, I keep extra cash on hand so he gets experience handling money and counting the change."
>
> —Nick, Coppell, Texas

Around age seven or eight you can start giving your children an allowance (which we will cover later) and let them handle their own money. As they get older, they will be ready to earn money, save money, and learn how to budget.

Twelve years and older

Children this age are capable of understanding anything you want to teach them about money. However, at this age they also start thinking they know everything! So dust off your thinking cap—you might have to use some creative teaching methods. Here are some ideas to get you started.

❀ Give them an allowance if you haven't started already.

- Open a checking or savings account and teach them how to reconcile their checkbook.

- Play games like Monopoly or Payday where money is handled and they have to think and make decisions similar to the real world.

- Show them the family budget and ask their input on difficult decisions.

- Talk about your investments at breakfast.

- Teach them the basics of investing and then let them invest money.

- Talk about taxes at dinner.

Take a Walk on Boardwalk

PERSPECTIVE

"I got my first taste of money playing Monopoly with my family. When I was little my dad would play nice and not take all my money, but as I got older, his competitive side came out. I always hated it when he won, but I learned a lot from his strategy and methods of buying land and building hotels."
—Jiles, Tucker, Georgia

Try to turn everyday experiences into learning opportunities. We don't recommend sitting your thirteen-year-old down on the couch and saying, "Okay, now we're going to discuss inflation." A better approach would be when your daughter's grandparents are over sometime, strike up a conversation about the price of shoes or a Coke when they were growing up. After your daughter's interest is piqued, you can slip in some informational tidbits about why things are much more expensive these days.

Why Teach Your Children about Money

Don't really consider yourself a teacher? (Well, if you have kids, you're now a teacher by default.) Don't feel like you're very good with money yourself? (You're showing signs of improvement by reading this book.) Does this whole teaching thing seem like a lot of time and energy you don't have to expend? Well, no matter what your excuse for not teaching your kids about money, just remember, they *will* learn about money somehow. Unfortunately, *what* they learn may not be all that wise. As parents, we must teach our children about handling money because:

- It is a necessary life skill.

- Teaching our children how to handle money is part of teaching them to be responsible.

- Children need to learn the value of money and the value of things it buys to function in our society.

❀ At some point, our children will be leaving home and making a living for themselves. (And as much as you love your child, you don't really want them coming back to live at home, do you?)

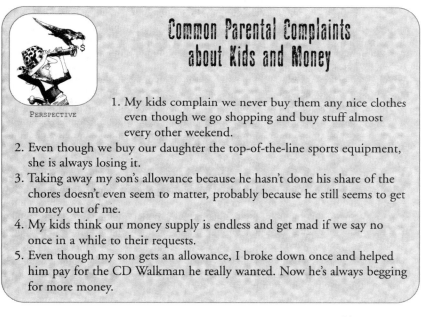

Common Parental Complaints about Kids and Money

PERSPECTIVE

1. My kids complain we never buy them any nice clothes even though we go shopping and buy stuff almost every other weekend.
2. Even though we buy our daughter the top-of-the-line sports equipment, she is always losing it.
3. Taking away my son's allowance because he hasn't done his share of the chores doesn't even seem to matter, probably because he still seems to get money out of me.
4. My kids think our money supply is endless and get mad if we say no once in a while to their requests.
5. Even though my son gets an allowance, I broke down once and helped him pay for the CD Walkman he really wanted. Now he's always begging for more money.

Allowances

Eric's mom is unloading groceries when he rushes into the kitchen and urgently says, "I need seven bucks quick. We're going putt-putt golfing and I don't have any money." But as she starts to object, he slam-dunks with, "But, Mom, Mrs. Smith is waiting in the car!"

At some point kids need money, and if you haven't decided ahead of time how you'll handle it when they come to you with a seemingly life-dependent need, you'll be on the spot to shell out the bucks. One way to handle it is to give an allowance. Since there are different ways to structure the allowance, we have described their differences to help you determine what works best for your family.

Ways to Provide Money to Your Children

1. Give money as needed

This method is not considered an allowance, for parents provide money whenever the child needs it. While this system puts the parent in the driver's seat of deciding if what the child wants money for is a worthy cause, it also has its drawbacks. Read this mom's struggles with giving money as needed:

"When Michael was little, I decided I would only give him money for things if I thought he deserved it and it was a worthy reason. But when he entered junior high, Michael wanted to do everything his friends were doing. That's probably when the begging started. I was regularly put in a position where I had to make immediate decisions. And because I was usually unprepared for his request, I gave him the money regardless, because I could never remember how much he'd already gotten that month, or if he'd done his chores sufficiently. Pretty soon, *I* was going broke!"
—Marsha, Greenwood, South Carolina

2. Paying for working at home

With this system, kids earn money by doing jobs at home. If kids want money, they can do a job, but if no work is done, no money is given. While kids are learning how to work and earn money with this system, there are still several drawbacks. Because this system is not a reliable source of income, the child doesn't learn how to budget or save. And while it eliminates most begging, it doesn't eliminate the times when the child needs immediate money and there's no time to complete a job.

Amazing Stories and Facts

Kids' Top Five Best Times to Get Money

(Don't let your kids read this!)

5. On their way out the door for school
4. When you're late for an appointment
3. When their ride is waiting
2. Right after you wake up in the morning and before your coffee
1. When you're in the shower

The major drawback can be seen in this mother's experience:

"We used to pay our kids to do work around the house, but it got harder and harder to get them to complete the family household responsibilities without paying them. A common response to asking them to clean their room or help with the dishes was, 'How much will I get paid?' "
—Jean, North Tonawanda, New York

3. Allowance tied to responsibilities

Most families use this type of system where a child is assigned household responsibilities but also receives a weekly allowance. When jobs are completed, the allowance is given, but if the jobs aren't done, then only some or no money is given. Essentially, the allowance becomes a form of reward and punishment. While it might seem like a good method on paper, learn from this mother's experience:

Are You Paying Bribes?

IMPORTANT REMINDERS

"If you don't take better care of the dog, you won't get your allowance this week!" Or, "I'll pay you $20 for every A you get this semester." It sounds like such an effective way to get your child to do what you want, but if you're using money to influence your child's behavior, it's called a bribe. Look out! A pattern of bribery teaches children they only have to control their behavior when there's a payoff. They learn nothing about responsibility.

"We set up an allowance system with our daughter to receive a certain amount a week, and her responsibilities included drying the dinner dishes, folding her own laundry, and cleaning her own bathroom. It worked well until she started folding only half her laundry, or instead of cleaning the whole bathroom she only wiped down her sink. We were forced to make frequent decisions about how much she should get since she only did part of the job. Then there were the times when she had a lot of homework and exams or went away on a trip and couldn't complete her responsibilities. It was too hard to be consistent, and she complained a lot."

—Jill, Battle Creek, Michigan

4. No-strings-attached allowance with supervised spending or free choice spending

With these two systems the child receives an allowance without any conditions. The difference is whether the parents supervise the spending of that money or they allow their child to use it however he or she wants. Here are examples of each:

"My wife, Linda, and I give our children a set amount of money each week but then require they tithe and save a portion of it. They are free to do what they want with the rest. We have friends who not only require their children to tithe and save but also determine for their children how much will be spent on clothes, activities, treats, etc. In doing this they feel they are teaching their children how to spend wisely."

—Frank, Kissimmee, Florida

Learning the Value of a Dollar

A TRUCKLOAD OF CLUES

"When Brad doesn't fulfill his chores and home responsibilities, we do not dock his allowance at all but discipline him in another way. We are trying to teach him how to budget and handle his money wisely. If we were to take away his allowance every time he did something wrong, he would never learn any money skills because he wouldn't have much money!"

—Jerry, Aliso Viejo, California

"Jim, my husband, and I have always given our children an allowance, then let them spend it on whatever they want and only intervene whenever they ask for help. We feel this builds their decision-making skills."

—Carla, Floussant, Missouri

5. No-strings allowance plus responsibilities

Parents incorporating this system give their children a set allowance plus require them to complete certain chores or responsibilities. This system differs from number three in that the chores are to be done *because* the child is part of the family. The allowance is always given and never withheld as punishment. This system allows kids to learn the skills needed to handle money properly while teaching them to be responsible, as well.

Why Choose the No-Strings-Plus-Responsibilities Allowance

You can choose whatever allowance system you want, but we're biased to the "no-strings-plus-responsibilities-allowance" and think it's the most effective method for teaching children money skills and responsibility. (And if you're anything like us, those two things are at the top of the list of "Things Our Children Should Learn.") Still unclear how it works?

Because your child is a member of your family, just like you, he:

❀ must accept his responsibility to help maintain the family. Just like Mom cooks and Dad mows the lawn, or vice versa depending on your family, he has family chores like feeding the dog or washing the dishes.

Money Doesn't Grow on Trees

PERSPECTIVE

"When I grew up, my brothers and sisters and I got an allowance, but we also had jobs we were required to do because we were part of the family. I was expected to keep my room clean, set the table, and take out the trash. If I wanted to earn extra money, there was a list of jobs and pay on the refrigerator that I could choose from. I think it was a great system and am raising my kids that way, too."
—Jon, Wheaton, Illinois

❀ should receive his share, be it a small portion, of the family's income.

But these two things should not be tied together or dependent on each other, because:

❀ if you withhold your child's allowance because he didn't do his assigned chores, he no longer has a dependable income with which to practice proper money skills. So while it may be a tempting way to get the lawn mowed, don't do it.

❀ withholding the allowance turns the child's chores into paying jobs which defeats the purpose of teaching him to be responsible to others. Yes, a paying job teaches responsibility, but the idea is to teach your child not just to be responsible because he is getting paid. He has these family chores because he is part of the family, just like he receives money because he is part of the family.

Cooperation

A TRUCKLOAD OF CLUES

"When my parents were trying to decide how much my allowance would be, we talked about what it would cover, and then they let me figure out how much I needed. Even though I didn't get the amount I came up with the first time, we worked through the numbers and finally decided upon an agreeable amount. I think it's so cool that they let me help decide!"
—Paul, Maple Grove, Minnesota

If you want to teach your kids the relationship between work and money, set up jobs separate from their family responsibilities that they can do for pay.

How Much Allowance?

Now that you've narrowed down what type of allowance you will provide your children, the burning question is, how much money should be given? If you're looking for a hard-and-fast answer, we hate to disappoint you, but we will give some guidelines to assist your decision making.

❀ Estimate how much you spend on your child weekly. Give him that amount plus extra if you want him to save and/or tithe.

❀ Decide what things the money will cover. Will your child be using it to buy clothes or just entertainment?

❀ Decide what you can afford.

❀ Discuss it with your child, but you should make the final decision.

❀ Consider what their friends receive, but don't try to "keep up with the Joneses."

❀ Increase the allowance amount to cover more basic needs as the child reaches his teens.

Allowance Rules

Kids aren't the only ones who need rules. In order for the allowance system to be successful, here are the rules we parents must follow:

1. When the allowance is started, explain it to the child so he understands how it works.

2. Both you and your child should agree in advance how much should be paid and what expenses it will cover.

3. Pay the allowance to younger children on the same day every week, but teenagers can receive it on a monthly basis to encourage budgeting.

4. After the allowance has been paid, *never* give your child more money. When he spends it, it's gone until the next payday.

5. Let your child choose how he will spend his money.

6. Don't use the allowance as a form of discipline or punishment.

7. Hold an annual review on his birthday to set the allowance and chores for the upcoming year.

Teens and Money

"When my family would go on a trip, my parents would give me and my two brothers a certain amount of money that we could spend however we wanted on the trip. But when it was gone, we wouldn't get any more. Inevitably my brother John would always spend his money the first day on candy. My other brother, Peter, would always spend a little every day. But I would hold out and wait until I found that one special thing I really wanted to buy."
—Steve, Minneapolis, Minnesota

Like Steve's parents, you might have children where one seems to spend with reckless abandon while the others show more responsibility. As your children reach the teen years, you'll be able to see which lessons about money sunk in and which ones went in one ear and out the other. And then again, you might be facing new money issues you hadn't even considered. Such is life with a teenager!

Keeping Up with the Joneses

Let's face it; kids learn by example, and no matter how many times you say, "Do this", but you do *that*, they will inevitably do *that*. Our point is, if you feel your kids are spending money trying to keep up with their pals, take a long, hard look at yourself to see if you are, too. If you are, make the adjustment before approaching your kids on this subject. But if deep down you're not trying to keep up with the Joneses but feel your kids are, take some time to walk in their shoes before talking with them about it. It's hard being a teenager these days with TV and movies having such a big influence. Teens are constantly bombarded with the message that they need new stuff. And since kids want more than anything to be accepted by their peers, it's hard not to want everything their friends have. The next time your daughter starts badgering you for more allowance because "everybody's wearing that but me," take a deep breath and be prepared to communicate with her about:

❀ jealousy—see Galatians 5:19–21

❀ envy—see Proverbs 14:30

❀ pride—see Proverbs 13:10; Proverbs 16:18

❀ idols—see Exodus 20:4

Don't Count Your Chickens before They Hatch...

A TRUCKLOAD OF CLUES

"When I turned eighteen, I had saved enough money for a down payment on a car and had a job to cover my monthly payments and car insurance. So I got a loan and bought a used car which I only drove for a month, because it broke down and needed a $300 car repair. I didn't have $300, because the bank still wanted its monthly payment, so I couldn't drive it for six months. Here I had borrowed money for a car I couldn't even drive!"

—David, Paige, North Dakota

Borrowing Money

Most teens are gung ho about buying a car the second they turn sixteen. So when you explain in your ever-so-tender way that there's no way on God's green earth that you will ever buy them a car, and you get the response, "Well, I'll just borrow the money from the bank! That's what you did," stop whatever you're doing. Go and get the paper and calculator, because it's time for a lesson in Borrowing 101. Here are the points to include in your syllabus:

A. Monthly payments
B. Interest on the money borrowed
C. Money must be paid back no matter what
D. Foreclosure on the loan

Encourage Saving

Some teens just don't like advice on how they should save their money. Trying to get them to save for college or a wedding can be like pulling teeth. So why not employ the same techniques that businesses use to get their employees to save for retirement? It's similar to the 401(k) plan, but we'll call it the save-and-match plan. Encourage your teens to save by offering to match a percentage of, or 100 percent of, the amount they save. For instance, give them fifty cents for every dollar they save. When they see how much quicker their money grows, they'll be more apt to save. This technique also prepares them for saving later in life when they have a retirement savings plan at work. Note: Make sure your children understand that this money is not to be used as an addition to the allowance but is going into their savings accounts.

Reviewing the Budget Together

Money has become such a taboo thing to talk about that parents tend to keep their income, expenses, and budget to themselves. Most teens have no clear understanding why their parents could afford to buy a new washing machine but won't buy them a new stereo. Or why this month their parents bought them a new video game but wouldn't buy it last month. Those teenagers who have an idea of where the family's income is spent each month and how much (or little) is left over will have a much greater appreciation for the fact that there just may not be enough left this month for them to get those new shoes they just have to have. So pick a day to sit down with your teens and go over the family budget. Allocate extra time, because this exercise will become a springboard for other questions about taxes, insurance, and deductions. Once your kids see that a huge chunk of your check is taken by FICA, even before you bring it home, they'll demand to know who in the world FICA is. Teens will also see clearly from a budget review that the money supply is limited, and sometimes difficult choices must be made about how to spend what is left over. Once you do a budget review, we suspect your life will become much less stressful as fewer demands are made on you for money.

It's
Really Mine

PERSPECTIVE

"*I like to earn my own money, because when I buy something, I know I really earned it, and it's really mine.*"
—Ted, fifteen years old, from Jaffrey, New Hampshire

Teens and Jobs

Most kids want to make their own money. But if you have a teen who would rather lie on the couch and watch TV, he might simply need some help figuring out how to make money. See the section titled "Common Jobs for Teenagers." Once he gets a taste of what it's like to earn his very own money to spend, he'll be sold. Or do you have a teen involved in several after-school activities and you're worried her grades will suffer if she takes on a job? We're not talking about a twenty-hour-a-week job, although that is certainly an option for those who have time. There are plenty of jobs that may only take a few hours a week but provide experience your child won't get doing anything else. And who knows? Your teen might decide she likes working more than taking karate, and at some point, you'll have to let her make her own decision.

Benefits for kids who work

1. They learn how to plan their time.

2. They must be prompt and dependable.

3. They learn to make choices.

4. They learn from failures and mistakes.

5. Their horizons are expanded.

6. They practice problem-solving skills.

7. They learn the value of money.

Common jobs for teenagers

While flipping burgers at the local fast-food joint is a good job, encourage your teens to get creative with skills or services they can provide others in their neighborhood or church. Handling their own businesses gives them experience in advertising, marketing themselves, setting their own price, being competitive, budgeting, and managing their time. Here's a list of common jobs teens can do in their neighborhood:

❀ Lawn mowing

❀ Car washing

❀ Window washing

❀ Housecleaning

❀ Paper route

❀ Raking leaves

❀ Lifeguarding

❀ Pet sitting

❀ Dog walking

❀ Snow shoveling

❀ Neighborhood camp

❀ Tutoring

❀ Making jewelry

Healthy Competition

AMAZING STORIES AND FACTS

"My first job was mowing lawns for my neighborhood. I printed out flyers on my computer advertising my service and put them in everyone's mailbox. I quickly developed a decent customer base, until the kid down the street started to undercut my prices! Then I had to get competitive. I cut prices, added trimming and raking services, and did more advertising. I still made enough money to buy the bike I wanted, but I had to be creative."

—Jacob, Pendleton, Indiana

❀ Sewing

❀ Party setup and cleanup

Questions to Ask Yourself

Answer these questions to help determine what areas your child might need some help or encouragement in handling money. Remember some of these are age-dependent. Don't expect too much too young.

1. Does my child frequently ask me for money? Why? Why not?

2. Does our allowance system work? Why? Why not?

3. Does my child understand how to budget? Why? Why not?

4. Have we set up a savings account? Why? Why not?

5. As parents, are we exemplifying good money skills? How?

6. Am I expecting my child to learn about money only by watching my example? Why? Why not?

7. Is my child showing signs of responsibly handling money? Why? Why not?

8. Has my child had any work experience? Why? Why not?

While these questions can be answered yes or no, take them one step further and answer why or why not. Then make the adjustments needed so your child will learn to handle money responsibly.

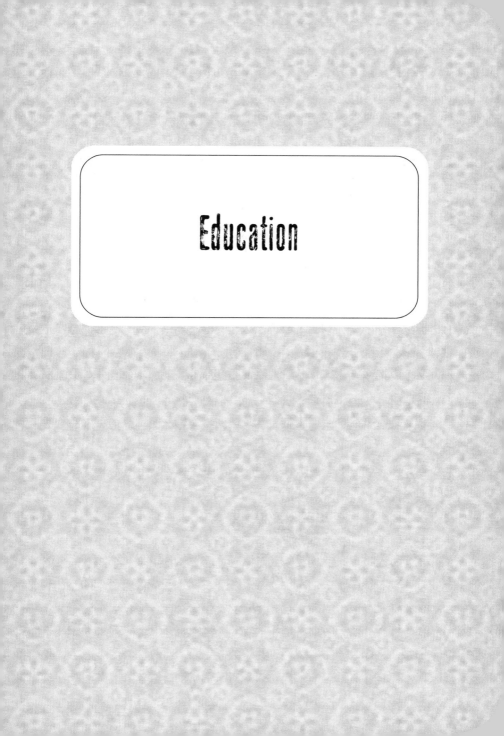

Education

A Payment Plan

Part of being a parent means being responsible for the education of your child. Whether you elect to homeschool Tyler or Brianna for a while or send him or her off to school, you know that a worthwhile education is one of the ways to give your son or daughter a great start in life. This includes decisions you make about placing your child in a public or private school for the preschool through college years.

An education is an investment that can be costly (but worth the price). Providing for the education of your child need not be a task as daunting as climbing the Adirondacks without the aid of rope or piton. The key is to plan ahead.

There are many ways to go about paying for education: using savings, government loans, scholarships, education IRAs, Roth IRAs, ROTC scholarships, the GI Bill. With so many "alphabets" in your soup, you'll need a plan of action to know which option(s) to choose. Need a hand with your plan? Glad you asked.

Seek and Accept God's Wisdom

Another part of being a parent involves praying for your child and any plans you have concerning him or her. Don't forget, God is a Dad, too—your heavenly Father. He wants to help His children. Seek God for wisdom to make good choices about your son or daughter's education. As James writes, "If any of you lacks wisdom, he should ask God, who gives generously to all without finding fault, and it will be given to him" (James 1:5). This includes being willing to submit your plans to Him.

There's an old saying, "You can lead a horse to water, but you can't make him drink." When God gives you wisdom (as this verse assures you that He will), it's up to you to act upon it. He won't force you to take His advice. If you do take it, wisdom is already in your grasp!

Pay Attention to Your Child's "Bent"

The Bible tells us to "train a child in the way he should go, and when he is old he will not turn from it" (Proverbs 22:6). That means actively watching to see in which way your child's gifts and talents will take him or her. This

A TRUCKLOAD OF CLUES

Start Early

"I started saving early. Early saving with compounded interest is important. In my daughter's situation, one issue for me was how to work with a divorce decree which says the other parent is to pay but does not. Again, I have found that prayer is the key."
—Joyce, Colorado Springs, Colorado

will have a decided impact on the type of school chosen and the money you'll need in order to make attending that school a reality for your child. If your child is musically inclined, he or she might benefit from a school that encourages the development of that talent. If your child is a computer whiz, that skill will require nurturing in an appropriate environment.

Keep in mind that every young person does not express a desire for higher education. Also, there is no guarantee that every family can afford to send their children to a tony preschool or college, even if they express a desire to go. Only you know your family's situation.

Tuition: Impossible

A TRUCKLOAD OF CLUES

For comic relief, have your college-bound son or daughter play the "Tuition: Impossible" game at the Kaplan site (http://www.kaplan.com) to test your financial planning savvy.

Research the Price of Tuition

Finding out how much education costs will give you a leg up on devising a plan for tackling the expense. Even if you have small children, you can still keep current on the price of tuition for colleges. You might start with your own alma mater, then work your way through some of the colleges in your area. Your local library and the Internet are two resources for research.

The average price tag is $100,000–$150,000 for a four-year education. Many private colleges cost more than that. You can pretty much expect that tuition will go up at least 10 percent each year. If your child is three years old now, you'll be facing a staggering amount of money for tuition by the time he or she is eighteen!

But, you may be thinking, *My little Egbert is brilliant. I'm sure that he will have a complete scholarship to go to college.* Well, perhaps that *could* happen. But. . .don't bank on it completely. Many schools offering financial aid still determine the family's portion of the tuition bill. That's why many parents elect to save money for their children's education or take out loans. Some even remortgage their homes to pay for college. Is that what you should do? For an answer to that, reread "Seek and Accept God's Wisdom." (In other words, that's something for you to pray about.)

Talk to Other Parents

Seek wise counsel from people who have sent their children to the preschool, middle school, high school, or college of your choice. See what plans

Education

95

they made and what the results of those plans were. If necessary, you might put your name on any waiting lists that they suggest (particularly for preschools; those slots fill up fast). The key here is *wise counsel*. That will mean taking with a grain of salt advice from disgruntled parents who chirp about how "worthless" the whole experience was or who try to tell you what you *should* do. After all, that decision is still up to you.

Talk to the Financial Aid Office

As you and your child consider appropriate colleges, keep in mind what your family can afford. If your child has selected a college, that college's financial aid office should be among your first contacts. Check with the financial aid director for eligibility requirements. Many financial aid services use a parent's income to decide how much aid to give. (See the section titled "Rescue Me!" for more information on applying for financial aid.)

For More Information

For more advice on paying for college, check out:

1. Your local library for financial aid sources.

2. Your financial planner for advice on ways to save (see also the "Saving for College" chapter).

3. Many Internet sources are chock-full of advice for parents of the college-bound. Some include:

❋ www.collegenet.com (a college search service)

❋ www.collegeview.com (a college search service)

❋ www.collegeboard.com

❋ www.embark.com (formerly known as www.collegeedge.com)

❋ www.kaplan.com (a site of many "talents," including Kaplan tests, advice on paying for college, and ways to choose a college)

THE BOTTOM LINE

Don't Forget

"When you're saving for college, don't forget to factor in the inflation rate each year. Otherwise, you may not save enough."
—Sam, a former high school guidance counselor

❋ www.usnews.com (the site of *U.S. News & World Report*, a good source for ranking colleges and discerning ways to pay for college)

❋ www.fafsa.ed.gov (FAFSA on the Web)

❈ www.ed.gov (the Department of Education's Web site—an excellent source for financial aid information)

If you do elect to do Internet research, check to see which sites are updated regularly. You'll want the most current information.

Your Plan So Far
What are your options? Circle those that apply.

1. Type of school you'd like for your child:

Exclusive preschool

Any preschool

Your denomination's elementary school

Private prep school

Arts and sciences academy

Ivy League college

Big Ten college

Any college

Other: _____

2. Steps you plan to take to make that desire a reality:
(List below or on a separate sheet of paper.)

_____

_____

3. How realistic is your goal?
(Only you can truthfully answer this.) Circle the number that fits.

1	2	3	4	5	6	7	8	9	10
Very realistic								Totally unrealistic	

Why?

_____

Education

4. What resources will you seek to make this goal more realistic?

College financial aid contributions

Internet Web sites for financial advice

Contributions from my extended family for my child's education

Other: _____

Saving for College

If you elect to go the savings route to pay for your child's education, most experts, nonexperts, and common sense will tell you that the sooner you start saving money, the better. In other words, if you're thinking about getting your child into an exclusive private preschool or *any* college, don't wait until he or she is of age before you start thinking about how you will foot the tuition bill. Remember: *Plan ahead.* How can you do that?

Start Saving Early

When you first decide to have children, you might begin to make a plan to save money for your children's education. This includes thinking about whether or not you can get little Tammi into that exclusive preschool that you just adored and how much you can set aside

AMAZING STORIES AND FACTS

The Voices of Experience

"I've always been told to start saving from the day they [your children] are born. Yikes—I guess since my son is already eight months old, I'm eight months behind on my savings!"
—Rebekah, Wheaton, Illinois

"I would advise any parent to start saving as soon as the child is born. Of course, there are many money concerns and bills throughout the school years, but every little bit would really help. Maybe a parent could start some type of monthly savings fund."
—Nancy, Colorado Springs, Colorado

monthly to do so. You can never be too early when it comes to saving money for your kids. Talk to a financial counselor about setting aside whatever discretionary income you can afford for an education fund.

However, don't worry if you cannot afford to save much or save anything at present. If you find yourself in this boat, trust your Savior to provide what you need when you need it (see Ephesians 3:20–21; Philippians 4:19).

Educate Yourself on the Coverdell ESA

Beginning in tax year 2002, parents and grandparents are allowed a $2,000 non-deductible contribution into a Coverdell ESA. This education savings account acts much like a Roth IRA, only it's like having a savings account for education. Earnings grow tax-free in the ESA, and withdrawals can be used for any schooling bills—from kindergarten to grad school. If used for any other reason, you'll have to pay a penalty.

Tax Credits to Consider

❀ The Hope credit provides a maximum credit of $1,500 per eligible student in any given tax year (100 percent of the first $1,000 of expenses and 50 percent of the next $1,000 of expenses). You can claim the Hope credit for any number of eligible students, and to qualify for the credit, the eligible student must be enrolled in one of the first two years of post-secondary education (generally, the freshman or sophomore years of college).

❀ The lifetime learning credit provides a maximum credit of $200 (20 percent of up to $10,000 of expenses) in any given tax year for expenses paid by the taxpayer. (The maximum credit was $1,000—20 percent of up to $5,000 of expenses—in 2002). The lifetime learning credit is not limited to students in the first two years of post-secondary education, and expenses for graduate-level degree work are eligible for the lifetime learning credit.

Please consult your tax advisor or IRS publication 970 (Tax Benefits for Higher Education) for more details.

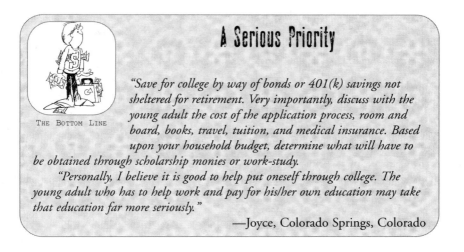

A Serious Priority

THE BOTTOM LINE

"Save for college by way of bonds or 401(k) savings not sheltered for retirement. Very importantly, discuss with the young adult the cost of the application process, room and board, books, travel, tuition, and medical insurance. Based upon your household budget, determine what will have to be obtained through scholarship monies or work-study.

"Personally, I believe it is good to help put oneself through college. The young adult who has to help work and pay for his/her own education may take that education far more seriously."

—Joyce, Colorado Springs, Colorado

Research the Roth IRA

Some parents go the "Roth Route" to pay for their children's education. Withdrawals are penalty-free if used for education. The Roth IRA is another spawn of the Taxpayer Relief Act of 1997. You can contribute up to $3,000 into a Roth IRA just as you can in a traditional IRA account. However, your investment earnings will be tax-free, but your contribution is not tax-deductible. This IRA, once called "the American Dream IRA," has its supporters and its detractors. You might ask your financial counselor or a banker for more information to gauge whether this plan is right for you.

Mull Over Mutual Funds

According to one financial planner quoted in *Newsweek* magazine's "How to Get into College" guide, parents should try to save $200 per month per child in a mutual fund. The key is to invest the money to gain a decent rate of return. Many parents go this route because the rate of return is higher than in a passbook account. A savvy financial planner can help you select the best mutual funds for wise investment.

Many parents who cannot afford $200 per month have elected to put away anywhere from $15 per paycheck to $50 per month, starting when the children were first born. The key is to put away what you can afford, not what someone says you *ought to be able to afford.*

IMPORTANT REMINDERS

Shoot for This

"Make it a goal not to spend more than your mortgage payment for each semester that your child is in college. There are hundreds of foundations out there with millions of dollars to pay the tuition and living expenses of enthusiastic, hardworking students. Don't pay a scam artist to "find" these scholarships for you; get to your local library or on the Internet to find the organizations that can help you out. The best reference book that I have found for this sort of thing is called Foundation Grants to Individuals. *You should be able to find this book in the reference section of your library."*

—Doug, Colorado Springs, Colorado

Select Other Savings Options

There are different options:

CDs

If your child will head off to college within a few years, you can elect to acquire a certificate of deposit (CD) for a term of six, twelve, eighteen, twenty-four, or thirty-six months with interest compounded daily. Certificates of deposit offer a fixed rate of return.

Savings bonds

Many parents go the Series EE-bond route. Income from these bonds is exempt from state and local income taxes. However, you can only defer federal income taxes until the bonds are due.

Other types of bonds

There are tax-free municipal bonds and zero-coupon bonds (the latter do not pay interest, but you're taxed as if you accrued interest). You'll need to make sure the bonds are fully mature by the time you need the money. Ask your banker or financial planner for more details.

Start Out with Stocks

This is an option to take several years before your child approaches college age. Stocks, however, are volatile. You may get great returns, but you could lose, as well. As your child gets older, consider switching to guaranteed sources, such as money market and short-term bond funds, as *Money* magazine suggests. Doing so will enable you to make your money "liquid" faster.

Picking the Right School

A TRUCKLOAD OF CLUES

"There are four children in our family. We told all of them that they would have to go to in-state universities to save money. Even though money is important, the most important consideration is picking the right college for the student. Students need to feel comfortable at their school. It needs to feel like home to them. My advice is to give your student options within your price range. Private colleges give more financial aid to outstanding students than state schools give. Also, start visiting colleges during the student's junior year. Applications have to be in early during the senior year."

—Linda, Batavia, Illinois

Some "Don'ts" to Keep in Mind

Don't put the money in your child's name.

Set up an education account in your name, rather than your child's. According to a Kaplan tip sheet, a school will expect 35 percent of a student's income to be used for tuition, but only 6 percent of a parent's savings.

Another reason for keeping the money in your name is to prevent the use of the money beforehand.

Don't neglect your retirement.

The old saying "Don't put all your eggs in one basket" obliquely applies here. Don't neglect your retirement plans [401(k) and such] to put all of your options to pay for college (loans, scholarships, etc.).

Don't feel that you have to save the whole amount.

Don't feel tied to saving for every penny of a four-year college education. You do have other options that you can consider. (See "Rescue Me!")

Don't be afraid to ask for help.

If you're not sure what forms you need to fill out or what investment plan is right for you, don't hold back on getting the help you need. Talk to a financial counselor, a banker, the financial aid director of your child's (or your) chosen school, or call the nearest IRS office or help line. You don't have to make guesses or feel foolish about asking "dumb" questions. The only dumb questions are those you have that remain unasked.

For Further Information

* www.money.cnn.com (for tips on saving for college)

* www.xap.com (XAP Corporation's college site has tips on financial aid)

* www.fastweb.com (another college site with tips for financial aid)

* www.bankone.com (or your own bank's Web site)

A TRUCKLOAD OF CLUES

Start Today!

"I don't think it's ever too early to start saving money for college. We inherited a small sum from a relative, divided it in half, and invested it in the children's names in mutual funds. This was done maybe fifteen years before they were ready for college, and when the time came, there was a nice sum to apply toward college expenses. I think it's important for children to also be saving, so if they get jobs at age fifteen or sixteen, a portion of it could be saved for college. We didn't encourage this last step and wish we had."

—Linda, Wheaton, Illinois

✿ www.estrong.com (for information on Roth IRAs)

✿ www.petersons.com (the company that publishes many college guides)

At the library, look for the latest financial aid guides (Barron's, Peterson's), or search for finance magazines like *Money*.

Rescue Me!

Once your family has decided on the type of college that best fits your budget, you'll need to consider options for payment beyond savings; namely, federal and state financial aid, loans, and scholarships.

According to the Department of Education in Washington, there is $60 billion available for educational aid. While you won't require *quite* that much for your child's education, you may want to invest the time to see exactly how much you *could* receive in aid.

The first place to start when thinking about financial aid for your education is the FAFSA (Free Application for Federal Student Aid) form. This is the form you need to fill out to get any federal assistance. The form helps to determine your EFC (Estimated Family Contribution). An equation determines your financial need:

Cost of attendance - Estimated Family Contribution = Financial need

You can submit a FAFSA through *FAFSA Express*. To download, head to www.fafsa.ed.gov or call 1-800-801-0576 (TDD 1-800-511-5806) to order *FAFSA Express* on disk.

THE BOTTOM LINE

I Sing a Song of Money

Money, money,
money, money!
Money!
Some people. . .got to have it!
Some people. . .really need it!
—Lyrics from the song
"Money, Money, Money" by the O'Jays

When you file, you are given an SAR (Student Aid Report) which lists your EFC. The Data Release Number (DRN) on the report allows the Federal Student Aid Information Center to send your SAR information to your chosen school. (Alphabet soup, anyone?)

When it comes to financial aid, remember two words: *File early* (anytime after January 1). If you have questions about filing, contact the Federal Student Aid Information Center, P.O. Box 84, Washington, DC 20044-0084. You can call them between 8 a.m. and 8 p.m. (eastern time), Monday through Friday at 1-800-4-FED-AID (1-800-433-3243). You'll need to call 1-319-337-5665 if you want a copy of your SAR.

Many online services also have an FAFSA you can download. (For a partial listing of services, see "For More Information" at the end of this section.)

Grants and Scholarships

When it comes to grants and scholarships, many think immediately of the song "The Impossible Dream" from *Man of La Mancha*. Although many grants and scholarships are dependent on a student's grades or financial need, there are quite a few available. The key is to find information on them and apply for them. Check with your college of choice or see your state financial aid office for in-state grant opportunities. See also "For More Information" for scholarship search databases. But keep in mind the Federal Trade Commission's "Project $cholarship $cam," a program that polices phony scholarship offers. (For the FTC's Web site, see "For More Information" on page 98. If you can, read the FTC's fact sheet on bogus scholarships before making a search for scholarships online.)

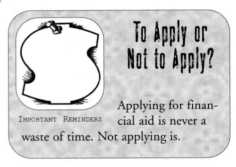

To Apply or Not to Apply?

IMPORTANT REMINDERS

Federal Financial Aid

There are many avenues for federal financial aid. The Expected Family Contribution (EFC) helps to determine your eligibility for Federal Pell Grants, Federal Stafford Loans, Applying for financial aid is never a waste of time. Not applying is.

Federal Supplemental Educational Opportunity Grants (FSEOG), the Federal Work-Study Program, and Federal Perkins Loans.

Pell Grants

Pell Grants are the largest federal need-based program. Like other grants, a Pell Grant does not have to be repaid. Millions of these are given out each year. For more information, contact: Federal Student Aid Information Center, P.O. Box 84, Washington, DC 20044 (301-722-9200).

FSEOG Grants

These are grants for students with extreme financial needs. You can get between $100–$4,000 per school year. The amount depends on your need and how much your school has. If you're in a study-abroad program, the maximum amount is increased slightly.

Direct Loans and FFEL Stafford Loans

You can also apply for direct loans through the William D. Ford Federal Direct Student Loan Program and Stafford loans through the Federal Family Education Loan Program (FFEL). These loans are subsidized and unsubsidized. Direct loans are disbursed from the government through your school while Stafford loans come from the lender to your school. After the money is paid for tuition and room and board, leftover money is given to you by check. You can decide on a number of repayment plans.

To apply for a loan, you have to fill out a Federal Stafford Loan Application as well as a promissory note. You can get both from your school or a state guaranty agency. For a Stafford loan, after giving your application to the school, the school's financial aid office will then send it to a lender. There are three different loan repayment plans. See your school or the U.S. Department of Education Web site for more details. You can also call 1-800-4-FED-AID (1-800-433-3243).

Parent Loans for Undergraduate Students (PLUS Loans) also fall under this category. These are loans parents can take out to pay for their son's or daughter's education. A good credit history counts for this type of loan.

Federal Perkins Loans

This is another type of low-interest loan for students in financial straits. You can borrow up to $4,000 as an undergraduate. If you go on to graduate school, your borrowing limit is $6,000. This loan is repaid to the school. To apply, contact the financial aid office of your chosen school. That school also sets the deadline for application.

AMAZING STORIES
AND FACTS

Desperately Seeking Assistance

"When Zack started college this past fall, we dutifully filled out those confusing financial aid forms only to find out that he was not eligible for any type of assistance because I made too much money! Me— a single mom who usually works two jobs just to pay the bills! Sooo, to put him though college, I had to work even harder getting freelance jobs to pay for his tuition. What is wrong with this picture?

"I couldn't get him to apply for scholarships. Next year I am going to insist he fill out some applications because it would really help!"

—Nancy, Colorado Springs, Colorado

Federal Work-Study Program

If you're itchin' to work your way through college, the work-study program is one way to do it. This program provides campus jobs at an average of ten to twenty hours per week. There may be a yearly cap on how much you can earn.

Other Loan Avenues

If you think Sallie Mae and Nellie Mae are Jed Clampett's daughters, think again. These organizations provide loans or loan consolidation for students. Other organizations include The Education Resources Institute (TERI) and EduCap Inc. (See "For More Information" for Web sites.) Contact Sallie Mae: 1-888-2-SALLIE (1-888-272-5543). Nellie Mae: 50 Braintree Hill Office Park, Suite 300, Braintree, MA 02184 (1-800-FOR-TUITION [367-8848]; fax: 1-800-931-2200).

State Financial Aid

Each state has its own financial aid agency. A high school guidance counselor or your local library can help you find the agency you need. You can also find plenty of help online. Run—don't walk—to the nearest resource!

CASHE

No, you're not looking at a typo for *cash*. This acronym stands for College Aid Sources for Higher Education. CASHE is linked to Sallie Mae's online scholarship service. You must fill out a Student Profile Form, which you can download from the CASHE web site. With this service, you can find information on fellowships, scholarships, grants, work-study programs, tuition waivers, loans, internships, competitions, and work co-op programs. You can get information within twenty-four hours. If you need more information on the CASHE program, visit the CASHE Web site (see "For More Information" below) or contact Edtech, Inc., P.O. Box 640, Kearney, NE 68848 (308-234-9700; fax 308-236-6013).

Military/Volunteer Programs

If you want to serve your country and go to college as well, look no further than these opportunities:

ROTC Scholarship Program

Students eligible for these scholarships serve four years in a branch of the service after graduating from college. They remain on reserve duty another two years.

Service Academy Scholarships

Students enrolling in military academies (i.e., the United States Military Academy at West Point; the Citadel) are qualified for various scholarships offered to outstanding cadets. If you're online, you might check your chosen school's Web site for details.

GI Bill

The government provides money monthly for education. To be eligible, a person has to serve at least two years. The money allotment increases after three years of service. Contact a recruiter for more details.

Volunteerism

There is another way to serve your country: acting as a volunteer to help others. Serving as a volunteer can qualify you for the President's Student Service Scholarships. College Board Online has a listing of places you can contact. Some of the Web sites are listed below. Contact your chamber of commerce, the United Way, or city hall for volunteering opportunities.

Neither a Borrower Nor a Lender Be?

A TRUCKLOAD OF CLUES

Many of us live by the maxim uttered by Polonius in Hamlet, *Act I, Scene III: "Neither a borrower nor a lender be; for loan oft loses both itself and friend, and borrowing dulls the edge of husbandry."* *But sometimes necessity (the high cost of college) breeds the need to do so. When in doubt about taking out a loan, pray!*

Aid for Minority Students

A few organizations that offer aid:

Bureau of Indian Affairs Higher Education Grant Program

Eligible Native American students can contact the Department of the Interior Bureau of Indian Affairs Office of Public Affairs, 1849 C Street NW, Washington, DC 20240-0001 (202-208-3711; fax: 202-501-1516).

Congressional Hispanic Caucus

Qualified Hispanic students can contact: Congressional Hispanic Caucus, 504 C Street NE, Washington, DC 20002 (202-543-1771; fax: 202-546-2143).

The United Negro College Fund

Over 1,000 scholarships are awarded yearly. To be eligible, you must attend a United Negro College Fund school. Contact the United Negro College Fund, Inc., 8260 Willow Oaks Corporate Drive, Fairfax, VA 22031 (1-800-331-2244).

Aid for the Handicapped
Here are just a few:

American Foundation for the Blind
Contact the American Foundation for the Blind, 11 Penn Plaza, Suite 300, New York, NY 10001 (212-502-7661; fax: 212-502-7777).

Alexander Graham Bell Association for the Deaf
Contact the Alexander Graham Bell Association for the Deaf, 3417 Volta Place NW, Washington, DC 20007-2778 (202-337-5220).

Disabled American Veterans Auxiliary National Education Loan Fund
Contact the National Education Loan Fund Director, National Headquarters, Disabled American Veterans Auxiliary, 3725 Alexandria Pike, Cold Spring, KY 41076 (606-441-7300).

For More Information
For fast online help, check out:

❋ www.fafsa.ed.gov (FAFSA on the Web)

❋ www.ed.gov/studentaid

❋ www.fafsa.ed.gov/fotw304/fslookup.htm (Federal School Codes used to complete the FAFSA)

❋ www.finaid.org/NASFAA (the scholarship database at the web site of the National Association of Student Financial Aid Administrators, NASFAA)

❋ www.collegenet.com (for financial aid questions)

❋ www.kaplan.com (the Kaplan home page)

❋ www.usnews.com (*U.S. News Online*; offers good advice for the college bound)

❋ www.ftc.gov (Federal Trade Commission home page; provides helpful information on companies offering bogus scholarships; you'll want to avoid those!)

❋ www.theoldschool.org (the Financial Aid Resource center—an excellent resource!)

❋ www.fastweb.com (boasts itself as the "Internet's largest free scholarship search")

❋ MOLIS Scholarships/Fellowships database (minority students)

* www.ed.gov/prog_info/SFA/StudentGuide (the financial aid guide of the U.S. Department of Education Web site)

* www.srnexpress.com (Scholarship Resource Network Express for scholarship search)

* www.Salliemae.com (Sallie Mae site)

* www.Nelliemae.com (you guessed it—Nellie Mae's site)

* www.teri.org (would you believe it—The Education Resources Institute [TERI] site)

* www.unitedway.org (volunteering info)

* www.servenet.org (volunteering info)

* www.impactonline.org (volunteering info)

* www.citadel.edu (Web site of the Citadel)

* www.usma.edu (West Point Web site)

* www.doi.gov/bureau-indian-affairs.html

* www.uncf.org (United Negro College Fund)

* www.afb.org (American Foundation for the Blind)

* www.dav.org (Disabled American Veterans Auxiliary site)

Don't forget search engines like:

* www.aol.com

* www.yahoo.com

* www.google.com

* www.teoma.com

Purchasing

Wise Use of Money

Money is a precious commodity, one you don't want to be foolish with. But, surprisingly enough, people spend more time planning and dreaming about how to spend their money than how to squeeze more out of their dollar. They don't realize that, more often than not, rich people aren't just making more money than they know what to do with, but they're being very careful about *how* they spend their money. Since money doesn't grow on trees, this chapter will help you get more bang for your buck.

Budget Wisely

We highly recommend setting up a budget of your income and expenditures if you haven't done it already. It's imperative that you know how much to allow for the basic necessities of life—groceries, utilities, gas, social activities (yes, going out is a basic life necessity), taxes, etc. The budget will serve as a guide for your spending and saving.

Our word of wisdom: Live within your means. Otherwise known as: Don't spend more than you make.

Spend Wisely

Money has a tendency to burn a hole in some people's pockets quicker than others'. And sometimes that hole can get really big—so big they can't even afford to buy thread to sew it up. We're talking about those who carry a balance on their credit card. We address this in the section titled "The Dangers of Credit."

Our word of wisdom: Don't carry a balance. You're wasting money and digging a hole that only gets harder and harder to get out of. Pay off your balance every month.

Think Wisely

Money is an important part of our lives, one you will do well not to ignore. But it's important not to let it control our lives. The Bible says it's not wrong to think about money; it's *how* we think about it that can be wrong. Our thoughts about money become a problem when we either worry about not having enough or we love and worship it more than God. The Bible has something to say about each of these:

> *"So do not worry, saying, 'What shall we eat?' or 'What shall we drink?' or 'What shall we wear?' For the pagans run after all these things, and your heavenly Father knows that you need them. But seek first his kingdom and his righteousness, and all these things will be given to you as well."*
>
> Matthew 6:31–33

"No one can serve two masters. Either he will hate the one and love the other, or he will be devoted to the one and despise the other. You cannot serve both God and Money."

Matthew 6:24

For the love of money is a root of all kinds of evil. Some people, eager for money, have wandered from the faith and pierced themselves with many griefs."

1 Timothy 6:10

Our word of wisdom: Keep your focus on worshiping God, not on yourself or what you buy.

Ways to Save Money

Competition between retailers is so high these days that they have to do some creative marketing and offer special deals to get consumers to buy from them. That is an advantage to us because it usually means we save money. But in order to catch some of these deals, you've got to stay sharp. We've outlined for you the major ways to save money and listed their pros and cons. From there, you can decide what methods for saving work best for you.

Coupons

Are you a coupon ripper or clipper? Do you rip coupons from magazines at the hairdresser or laudromat, leftover newspapers, and anywhere you can find them, and then carry your envelope of ragged-edge coupons to the grocery and hand a wad to the cashier as you check out? Or do you clip coupons with scissors and organize them nicely into a filing system? Whatever your style, coupons are a great way to save money. They're almost like free money. *Almost* being the key word of that sentence. To make sure you're getting the best use out of your coupons *and* your money, we've outlined the pros and cons to using coupons.

Pros

❀ You save money. We realize you already knew that, but we had to list it as the number one pro.

❀ Coupons are everywhere—the newspaper, flyers in the mail, in magazines, at the grocery store. You can even buy coupon books.

❀ Some stores accept competitors' coupons. Some even have been known to double competitor coupons! What a deal when the store you wish had a coupon honors the competitor coupon you're holding.

Coupons are marketing genius. Companies are enticing you to buy their products or services by offering you a discount. It really is a win-win situation for both the company and the customer. Their product is bought and you save money. But sometimes, all is not as it seems. Here are the cons of coupons:

Cons

❀ The deal is not as good as it looks. The coupon reads SAVE 40¢! But when you look at the fine print, you have to buy three! That's not much savings.

❀ Even with the coupon, the product is still more expensive than others. Just because the coupon says 50 cents off doesn't mean the product is the best buy. Be sure to price compare no matter what.

THE BOTTOM LINE

Proper Pronunciation:

We want to set the record straight on the proper way to say "coupon." Some people pronounce it Q-pon, while others say KOO-pon. According to Webster's dictionary, BOTH pronunciations are correct!

❀ You tend to buy things you don't need. Remember, just because the coupon makes it a great deal doesn't mean you necessarily need to buy it.

❀ You spend money to get coupons. If you buy the Sunday newspaper simply to clip coupons, you have to clip quite a few to make up the amount you spent on the paper. The same is true for coupon books you have to buy. Be sure to look through them first and read the fine print. Sometimes the coupons have specifications that would hinder you from using many of them.

❀ The coupon is too good to be true. Be careful about services that offer incredible deals. If it seems too good to be true, it probably is. Learn from our experience:

> "I received a coupon in the mail for a free replacement window with the purchase of one. Since we were getting bids to have our windows replaced, I called the company. But when they gave me the quote, it was more expensive than other quotes I'd received. So when I mentioned having a coupon for a free window, the salesman said, 'Oh yeah, I figured that into the quote already.' Some deal!"
>
> —Christine, Wheaton, Illinois

Use Coupons Wisely

Your best bet for making the most of coupons is to clip coupons for products and services you would normally purchase. That's not to say never clip a coupon for a

Coupon Frenzy

The envelope with a handful of coupons offering great deals on carpet cleaning, new windows, having your air ducts cleaned, a Princess Diana figurine, new cookbooks, and the like just arrived in the mail. Your heart begins to race, your palms get moist, and your breathing picks up at the thought of saving sooo much money. But take a step back and do a reality check. Do you really need your air ducts cleaned? Will you really use new cookbooks—especially one a month? And where are you going to put that figurine? Think first before the coupon frenzy takes over.

new or different product. Just be careful about purchasing items just because you have a coupon. But if you've been wanting to try that new pizza place and they sent you a coupon, by all means, use it! One more tip: Make sure the companies you have a coupon for are reputable and always shop around first.

Sales

The really savvy shoppers are those who know when and where the sales are and never pay full price for anything. But then again, they shop *a lot*! If you can't or don't want to commit that kind of time to the mall but still want to get great deals, read on. We've put the sales information at your fingertips, so you only have to go shopping when there are deals to be had.

Know when the sales are

Stores don't just decide willy-nilly to have a sale this week. There is a pattern to their markdowns. You just have to know when they are. Common sale times are:

❋ Postholiday sales. You can stock up big for next year if you wait 'til after the holiday to buy Christmas decorations, Easter baskets, Valentines, July 4th supplies, and such. But our advice is to shop early postholiday to get the best of what's on sale.

❋ End-of-season sales. Stores are marking their stuff down to sell it and make room for the next season's incoming merchandise.

❋ Preseason sales. This is an incentive to get you out shopping for the new season. These sales are not as good as the end-of-season sales.

❋ White sales. Most major department stores have a white sale in January and August every year. So wait to buy sheets or towels until then.

❀ End-of-the-month sales. Some stores even have end-of-the-month sales to make room for new inventory.

Keep your receipt

If you buy something and it goes on sale or is marked down even more within a couple weeks of your purchase, take your receipt back. Most stores will honor the new price and give you money back.

Outlet Malls

Outlet malls might be the greatest invention ever for the shopaholic. Where else can you get rock-bottom prices on clothes, sporting gear, household items, and just about anything? But just like everything else in this chapter, there are definite pros and cons to outlet shopping.

Pros

❀ You can get some really great deals on quality products. And when the outlets have sales, look out—you might find the "deal of the century"!

Unfortunately, while this is a very fine pro, be aware there are several cons to shopping at an outlet.

Cons

❀ Not all outlets are real outlets, especially in outlet malls. Don't be fooled. Just because a store is located in an outlet mall doesn't mean it is an outlet. Many stores place themselves there to take advantage of the shopping frenzy that people get into when they enter an outlet mall.

❀ Price tags may lie. When you look at a price tag and the suggested retail price is on top and then the store's list price is below it, it always looks like such a great savings. But keep in mind that the suggested retail price is just that—suggested. Stores can inflate those prices to make their list price look like a better deal.

❀ Quality is not always the best. Many companies send their seconds or flawed items to outlets, so make sure you examine the item before you buy it. Other stores actually make clothes and products of lesser quality to be sold in their outlets.

❀ Prices are not always cheaper. Many people assume that because it's an outlet, the prices will be cheaper. But do your homework ahead of time and know what things cost before you buy.

❀ You have to pick through a lot of stuff to find what you want. But if you're on a mission to get the best deal, it won't matter how hard you have to look.

Tips for Outlet Shopping

1. Know product prices in everyday stores. So what if it's a name-brand white turtleneck for $30, marked down from $50? If you can get a white turtleneck at your local department store for $15, this isn't such a great deal. Unless you tell people, no one is going to know whether the turtleneck you're wearing is designer or not. Don't worry; no one will be reaching down your shirt to check the tags.

2. Avoid outlet fever (unless you can afford it). It is very similar to coupon frenzy. As you open the door to the store, your heart rate and breathing pick up, your eyes frantically scan the room for which rack to pounce on first, and thoughts of anything else but getting good deals leave your mind. Pretty soon, your arms are loaded down as you make a run for the cashier who happily swipes your credit card before you have a moment to reconsider.

3. Avoid buyer's remorse. Our best advice for you who tend to buy things just because they're on sale and then realize when you get home that you don't even like them is, *Keep your receipts.* And make sure you understand the return policy. At some outlets the sale is final, especially if the items are on sale.

It Wasn't Even Cute

A TRUCKLOAD OF CLUES

"While on a trip, I was shopping at a Ralph Lauren outlet and couldn't believe they had wool sweaters for $15! Even though the only color in my size was orange, it was such a great deal, I couldn't pass it up. When I got home I realized the sweater wasn't even cute. I wore it once with the intention that I would bring orange back into fashion but then wished I hadn't wasted my money."
—Julie, Overland Park, Kansas

Wholesale Clubs

If you're into megabuying and megasaving, then a wholesale club might be right up your alley. These companies are dedicated to bringing their members the lowest possible prices on quality name-brand merchandise. Their no-frills approach keeps their expenses to a minimum, and they then extend their savings to their customers. It's really amazing what you can buy at one of these clubs. They offer groceries, apparel, jewelry, office supplies,

Top Three Wholesale Clubs

THE BOTTOM LINE

1. Sam's Club
2. Costco
3. BJ's Wholesale Club

janitorial supplies, electronics, household products, books, videos, business products, and some are even starting to sell gas at discount prices. It almost sounds too good to be true! But, alas, before you decide you can't live without shopping here, look at the pros and cons.

Pros

❀ By far, the pro to shopping at a wholesale club is buying quality products for less money. What could be better than that? Just keep in mind, the prices are cheaper for a reason. You have to be able to deal with the cons to get the deals.

Cons

❀ It ain't free. To become a member you have to pay a yearly membership, which is usually around $35. Before you join, try to go with someone first to make sure you like it and will actually shop enough to make your $35 worth it.

❀ You have to buy in bulk. And we're not talking just the jumbo size. We mean cases of pop and the twenty-four pack of paper towels. Now for some people that may not be a problem. But if you have limited storage space, where in the world are you going to keep all that stuff? You might get some good deals, but if you have to buy another freezer or build a shed to accommodate it, you might want to redo the math on how much money you're actually saving.

❀ It's a warehouse. Expect your shopping experience to be very dull. They haven't rolled out the red carpet. In fact, there isn't any carpet at all. And the products are displayed pretty much the way they came off the truck—on pallets and in boxes. Needless to say, there isn't much "atmosphere" to make you feel good. But then again, you're trying to save money, not have an "experience."

❀ It could be far away, depending on where you live. Most people live in neighborhoods not near warehouses, so you might have to drive a long distance to get there.

❀ You need time to shop. Remember, you'll be shopping in a warehouse. Don't plan on a quick run in for milk or a snack—leave that for the local stores. And by all means, don't take your one-year-old who needs constant attention, or you'll pull your hair out.

Don't let all the cons keep you from joining. We just want you to have a realistic view of what shopping at a wholesale club will be like.

Cash, Check, or Charge?

If you're reading this book, you probably bought it. But *how* did you buy it? Did you pay cash, write a check, or charge it on a credit card? There are advantages and disadvantages to each method of payment. Are you aware of them all?

Cash Pros

❀ You always know up front how much cash you have to spend. Just check your pocket.

❀ You can't go into debt as easily. Let's face it—if you don't have the money in your hand, you can't buy that object of your desire.

❀ It's accepted everywhere. No one is going to turn down cold, hard cash as payment for anything.

❀ You don't need any form of ID to use cash. No one needs to check and see if the money you're using is yours or make sure you're a reliable person. Money does all the talking.

But just as there are so many great things about cash, there are also cons.

Cash Cons

❀ When it's gone, it's gone. If you need money for something but don't have any cash, you're stuck. The guy at the gas station isn't going to take an IOU for the gas no matter how much you plead that you're good for the money.

❀ Bills and coins can be bulky. It's pretty noticeable if you're carrying around a wad of cash in your pocket. It can weigh down your purse or make your behind look so lopsided that all the pickpockets in the area take notice and spring into action, which leads us to the next point. . . .

❀ It can get stolen, or you can easily lose it. And when cash is gone, there's no way to prove it was yours.

❀ You can't Internet shop with cash.

Check Pros

❀ It's just like money. It's a universally accepted IOU note saying you're good for the money and the bank will pay it.

❀ They're easy to carry around. That little folder slips right into your pocket or purse.

❀ It's easy to keep records of your spending. The place to record is built into the back of the book. You just have to get in the habit of writing down when you use a check.

❀ Checks are accepted almost everywhere.

Check Cons

❀ You need some form of ID, like a driver's license, to confirm your identity.

AMAZING STORIES AND FACTS

Hairy Haircut

"It was the first time I had gone to this hairstylist to cut my hair. When I went to pay her, I realized I hadn't brought any cash with me, so I asked if I could go find an ATM station and come back to pay her. But she didn't like that idea and asked if there was anyone who could bring me some money. I had to sit there for a humiliating hour until my sister could bring me some cash."
—Pam, New York, New York

❀ If you forget to record a check, it throws off your records.

❀ There are charges for overdrawing your account. It could be several weeks before you realize you're overdrawn and have accumulated charges.

❀ Checks can be easily lost or stolen.

❀ You can't Internet shop with a check.

Credit Card Pros

❀ All you have to do is sign your name. Not carrying any money? No worries!

❀ Credit cards are accepted almost everywhere.

❀ You don't need any ID to use one.

❀ You can buy something now and have a month before you have to pay for it.

❀ You can rack up frequent flier miles, points toward free gas, a car, or items at your favorite store.

❀ You can Internet shop.

❀ Credit cards are easy to carry.

IMPORTANT REMINDERS

Debit Dork

"The kid at the checkout line had already bagged all my groceries when I realized I had my wallet, but I didn't have my credit card (it was sitting on the kitchen table at home), nor my checkbook (in the desk), and I was out of cash. Staring at my open wallet as if money would appear, I saw my debit card. Whew! But could I remember the pin number? After a few deep calming breaths, it came back to me. I paid and left but forgot to write down that I had used the card and spent $150!"

—Colleen, Fayetteville, Arkansas

Credit Card Cons

❋ They provide a false sense of money.

❋ Charges and late fees for not paying the bill on time are high.

❋ They are easily stolen or lost.

❋ Some card companies require a yearly fee to use their card.

Debit Cards

They look like credit cards but work like a check and act like money. They're the newest kid on the block, and they're called debit cards. But while they do have their advantages, be careful. Since there's no place to record your purchases, it's easy to lose track of when you use your card. And while it's instant cash, your account is immediately debited. There is no grace period as with a credit card, so make sure the cash is in the bank.

There are pros and cons to each of these methods of payment. So whether you choose cash, check, charge, or debit, the key to staying out of trouble is to know how much money you have in the bank. If you keep good records of what you spend and when, then you won't write any bad checks or overcharge your credit card.

The Dangers of Credit

There are certain rules that credit card companies have set up, and if you live within those rules, you'll be in the clear and you won't lose a dime. But if you get careless (which they secretly hope you will) and don't pay off your balance, the card companies start chanting, "Cha-ching!"

Know Your Card

We know how incredibly boring that fine print on the back of the credit card statement is, so for all you folks with bad eyesight or little patience, we took the liberty of reading it and condensing it for you. Although almost bored to tears (sometimes we wondered if they wrote the fine print the way they did so no one would read it), we managed to trudge through it because we know how important it is to understand the card rules before spending any hard-earned cash. Here are some of the common fees you could be charged if you're not careful.

A TRUCKLOAD OF CLUES

Waive That Annual Fee

To get your fee waived, call the credit card company and explain that you have been a good customer and don't see why you should have to pay an annual fee when so many cards are available without one. Be ready to drop their card and sign on with another company if they call your bluff.

Annual Fee

Some credit card companies charge you a yearly fee just to carry the card in your wallet. For the average run-of-the-mill Visa or MasterCard, it's about $20, and $50 for a gold card. But don't be ripped off any longer! You can get the fee waived. (Bet you're listening now!) Competition in the credit card business is getting fierce, so companies are showing a willingness to drop the annual fee for customers they like. (Hopefully, that will be you.) If you've been a good customer (which we're sure you are), odds are they will drop the fee, and you will have earned back enough to pay for this book and buy one for a friend!

Interest Fee

If you are late paying your credit card bill by one day, you will be charged an exorbitant amount of interest on your balance. The APR (annual percentage rate) on your card can be up to 21 percent! So do whatever it takes to make sure you are paying on time.

THE BOTTOM LINE

Are You a Revolver?

The credit card company refers to the folks who continually carry a balance on their credit card as *revolvers*.

Late Fee

This fee is pretty much what it sounds like. You get dinged if you're late in paying your balance. Late fees are usually estimated at 2 percent of your outstanding balance if you don't make at least a minimum payment by the due date shown on the bill. This fee is in addition to the interest fee you'll be charged.

Exceeding Your Limit Fee

While some cards become invalid if you try to exceed your limit, others let you keep spending and then charge you for it.

Other Fees

If you're the perfect customer, paying your bills on time and never getting charged any interest, the credit card company doesn't make much money off of you. Well, some card companies have wised up and now charge people like you a small fee every time you use the card. But if you're the not-so-perfect customer and run up interest charges or use your card frequently, which generates fees paid by the merchants who accept the card, you escape this fee (don't be fooled; you're getting charged elsewhere). Getting dinged with every purchase? It's time to find a new card.

Grace Period

After reading about all these fees, it's hard to believe that any credit card could have a bright side. But most cards do by extending you a grace period. After you're billed, you have twenty-five to thirty days before interest on the money you've spent starts accruing. It's basically a free loan. And if you make your purchases right after your billing date, you can stretch that loan time to nearly two months! But check the fine print on your credit card. Some companies don't have grace periods at all but start charging you interest from the date of a purchase if you carry a balance from the previous month. That's something you don't want to find out after the fact!

Trapped

PERSPECTIVE

"After we were first married, we bought a house but didn't have many furnishings. But that didn't matter. We had our credit cards! We bought a new dining room set and new appliances. But then we had to have some new dishes, TV, and an entertainment center. We limped along for a while paying the minimum balance on our card, but that didn't stop us from going on a vacation to Hawaii. It was fun until we couldn't pay our electric bills and had to file for bankruptcy. We thought we could live like we had money, but it came back to haunt us."

—Donna, Irvine, California

Read and Heed

Read the fine print before making any purchases. Don't just open up the envelope holding the latest card proclaiming a low 12.5 percent interest rate, sign your name, and go on a spending spree. The fine print is fine for a reason—they're hoping you won't take the time to find out that you're charged for every purchase made, and the second you miss a payment they'll slap you silly with fees. While we condensed the fine print for most cards, you need to read about your own card and know when and why you're going to be charged.

It's Really a Loan

To put it plain and simple, a credit card is basically a short-term loan. When you're issued a card, you're given a credit limit—a predetermined amount the company will allow you to spend/borrow for one month. So for example, if your credit card limit is $5,000 and you buy $500 worth of merchandise, you have $4,500 left in credit. When you repay the $500, you again have $5,000 available. As you use the card, you're constantly borrowing against your limit and repaying the money. It's *how* you repay that loan that determines whether or not you're living in the danger zone.

Easy Money

PERSPECTIVE

"I was just out of college and needed to buy some new clothes for my first job. The credit card seemed like the easiest way to get what I wanted now, and I figured I could pay it back after a couple of paychecks from my new job. But a couple months went by, and I was still paying the minimum balance because I didn't realize how much life's basic necessities would cost and how little would be left over. I finally paid the balance off after two years, but when I see how much I paid in interest, it still makes me mad."

—Matt, Las Cruces, New Mexico

Staying Out of Danger

If you would rather keep your money than give it to the credit card companies, then we suggest paying off your balance in full each month so that no interest charges will accrue. If this is how you intend to manage your credit card payment, then be sure to select a credit card that has no annual fee. And don't worry about what the APR is. It won't matter because you pay off your balance in full each month and never have to pay any interest. The key to paying off your balance every month? To put it simply: Don't charge more than your monthly income. We know how tempting it is when you see something you really want to just put it on the Visa and worry about paying for it later. But later tends to become forever, especially if you buy several things you want. It becomes harder and harder to pay things off because you usually don't have any more money later than you do now.

Watch Out for the Trap

Oh, the commercials make credit cards look so good. They tout their card as the answer to all your needs. You can fill your new home or apartment with furniture, go on an incredible trip, eat out as much as you want, and fill your closet with the trendiest clothes—all with no worries. The money is at your fingertips. But, buyers beware! The trap is lurking. Yes, you can do these things, *but* (there's always a but, isn't there?) if you don't have the money to pay the balance, then they have you by the jugular. Yeah, you might have what you want now, but you'll end up paying four to five times more than the item was worth over the course of time, not to mention an unbelievable amount of money in interest and possible late fees. Plus, if you ever decide there's anything else you want to buy, you're going to have to use the credit card and rack up more fees because all your money is going to paying off an already existing balance. The commercials look so good because the credit card companies want you to spend a fortune on your card. This ensures them a steady income from the interest you pay.

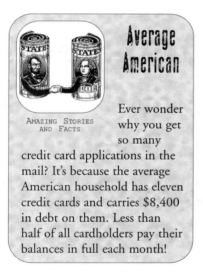

Average American

AMAZING STORIES AND FACTS

Ever wonder why you get so many credit card applications in the mail? It's because the average American household has eleven credit cards and carries $8,400 in debt on them. Less than half of all cardholders pay their balances in full each month!

Cost of Carrying a Balance

The cost of carrying a balance can mean big bucks to the credit card company and a big loss for you. Let's say you ring up $3,000 on your credit card which charges 17.5 percent interest. If you decide each month to only pay the $10 minimum payment and roll the balance into the next month, it will take you a whopping thirty-three years to pay back the $3,000, and you will end up paying over $6,000 dollars in interest!! It will be even more money if you continue to use the card and rack up more charges.

Luxury Fever

Luxury fever is a highly contagious condition that affects one's heart and wallet. It infects millions of Americans every year. It can be deadly—financially, that is—and it's easily caught if you're tempted to carry a balance on your credit card.

How does one catch it? When our need to impress others becomes so great that we'll spend whatever it takes to look like we've got money and the goods to prove it. When we give in to the lie that we need to have things now if we're going to be happy.

Self-diagnosis

Ask yourself: "Are there things I'm buying now because I won't wait until I have the money?" "Am I using my credit cards to the point that I'm carrying a balance I can't pay off?"

Immunization

A strong desire to please God rather than ourselves or others. Regular boosters required. Regular boosters of prayer and reading God's Word are needed to keep your spending on track.

Treatment

If you do suffer from luxury fever and have overspent yourself, first commit your situation to God in prayer. Find help in dealing with debt and commit to paying off your loans and not overspending again.

Are You in the Danger Zone?

To help you determine how close you are to the credit card danger zone, we've outlined some questions to ask yourself:

❀ Have you established a spending budget?

❀ Do you put a portion of your income into savings?

❀ Do you often spend near your credit limit?

❀ Do you use multiple credit cards to make purchases?

❀ Do you carry a balance?

❀ Why are you not paying off your credit card(s)?

HELP FROM ABOVE

What Do You Love?

God cares about your decisions. The Bible says: "Do not love the world or anything in the world. If anyone loves the world, the love of the Father is not in him. For everything in the world—the cravings of sinful man, the lust of his eyes and the boasting of what he has and does—comes not from the Father but from the world. The world and its desires pass away, but the man who does the will of God lives forever" (1 John 2:15–17).

Debt Management

Consumer Credit Card Debt

When it comes to consumer debt, you can describe the problem in a lot of different ways.

❈ It's too easy today to get credit cards.

❈ This generation wants in their twenties what their parents earned by their forties or fifties.

❈ We don't know how to deal with delayed gratification anymore.

❈ We live beyond our means as a way of life.

All of them and more are true. You can hardly open a news magazine without finding an article about it. Consumer debt is at an all-time high. Some sources say that many people in their twenties owe twice as much in terms of consumer debt as their yearly income. We have lived beyond our means, plainly and simply.

The debt industry (and that is really what it is, not a credit industry) has worked hard, and their work has paid off. They have advertised. They have communicated with us. They have shown us pictures of pretty people in exotic places who got there because they were willing to owe a company whose only reason for existing is to get people to buy what they cannot afford.

They show us horrible emergencies that could wipe us out. They show us improvements on our homes. They show us a better life than the one we can now afford. They tell us that we can have it now. They show us a shortcut to tomorrow's life without working through the night to get there. All we have to do is owe them what we borrow. . . plus some.

And so we buy a car

AMAZING STORIES AND FACTS

An Interesting Fact

If you tune in to country music or if you've watched the movie *Deep Impact*, you may have heard a song titled "The Hole" (performed by Randy Travis). The idea for this song originated with a financial concept related to debt management. If you read much material about debt management, sooner or later you'll come upon the phrase "You can't dig out of the hole," meaning you can't borrow your way out of debt. One of the writers thought that concept was cool enough to base a song on it, and the song made it to the top ten. Who knew a financial concept could spawn a country song!

costing $15,000 and over six years pay $27,000 for it—and it makes sense to us! We buy a $75,000 house and over thirty years pay $125,000 for it. We rack up $3,000 on this and that for the new house and over a few years pay $5,000 for the old thises and thats that we sold at the garage sale.

They have convinced us that it is a natural way of life. Work hard? Save up? Wait until you have the money? Why, when they can let us have it now?

Loan Consolidation

Another way that lenders have capitalized on our struggle in this debt trap is to offer us new loans to consolidate our old ones. Some say the typical person over his head in debt has many as seven credit cards. Just keeping the envelopes

IMPORTANT REMINDERS

Beware

Chances are you get lots of unsolicited (unasked for) mail offering you some kind of financial deal. Maybe you throw them away without opening them. Maybe you put them in a pile that grows every day. Maybe you open every one of them and end up more confused than if you had left them sealed. Maybe you open them, understand them completely, and don't need to be reading this book at all (why do you open them if you understand all that stuff?). Whatever your level of understanding, here are some things to be careful about.

1. If it sounds too good to be true, it probably is.

2. If you can't find an interest rate in obvious sight, then it's probably not a good interest rate.

3. If they are offering you something free of charge, then they are making their money somewhere else. Make sure you know where they are making their money.

4. Make sure you know what fees will be charged.

5. Often companies who are offering you a less-than-good deal will disguise that fact by making things look a bit confusing, like it's so far above your basic understanding that you don't get it. It's not. Don't fall for it.

opened and the bills paid on time requires a certain amount of energy.

So there are lenders that will lend you the money to pay off those credit cards (and often at a more reasonable rate), and then you can make one simple payment to them. You save the interest and you save the stamps.

You will probably also increase your debt immediately because they will charge a bit for. . .for. . .for. . .well you might not be sure what for, but according to them, there is one to three thousand dollars that it costs them to. . .to. . .to. . .well, to do the paperwork or something. This might be worth it to you to get your debt organized. Just make sure you go in with your eyes open. If you're borrowing more to try and get out of debt, remember: You can't dig out of a hole.

If you choose to consolidate the loans that you have, be careful of this: You have only organized your debt; you haven't released yourself from it. What are you going to do with that extra $100 or $200 a month that you saved by consolidating? Don't increase your debt further and eat up that money with more credit card bills. If you consolidate your bills, let it be the beginning of borrowing nothing further, not just a step up debt mountain.

Also be careful when the salesman (called a loan officer or a customer service representative) adds up the total and then says, "And while you're doing it, do you want to throw in a few thousand more to help get over the hump?" It sounds good. You're borrowing anyway, after all. But if you do it, then you've increased your debt again, and you're still going backward whether it feels like it or not.

Debt or Credit Management Companies

Another industry that has arisen because of our society's penchant for borrowing is the debt management industry. These companies, many nonprofit, have taken a twist on collections. They are like a voluntary collections agency for people who feel out of control debtwise and want to get back in control. Some names you might recognize are Genus Credit Management and United Family Services (through United Way).

This is how it works. You go to them with all your credit card debt. Before you call, you might as well gather your last bill for each card. They will need your credit card number, the company name, the total balance, and the required payment. Then they will figure out what your payment would be if all the interest rates were reduced to a certain percent, often around 9 percent. If most of your credit cards are at the 18–22 percent mark, then the monthly savings to you could be substantial.

Next, they go to each of your credit card companies. They already have an agreed interest rate with most of these companies. If they don't, for instance, with small or regional companies or banks, then they'll negotiate with them individually

Collections

Have you ever talked to a bill collector? He or she may either be with a collection agency hired by the company that you owe, or he may be a person just like you that has been hired to sit at a phone and make calls and read a script. He has no particular interest in you. His opinion doesn't change your position or worth in the least. You are not in worse shape because he called you.

But that's not what it will feel like. Collection is a difficult and sometimes dirty business. The most popular techniques sometimes involve bullying and almost always involve shame. In his call you are immediately positioned as the enemy. He catches you off guard. He calls you at the worst time. There are even laws written specifically to legislate how much these people can harass you before it's just too much.

If you are facing the harassment of collection in some way, take a breath and make a plan of how you are going to repay your debts. Explain your plan to them and get off the phone. Always feel free to say, "I'm doing the best I can at this point to be responsible for my choices."

And remember, that person on the other end of the line or at the front door has no magic power over you. Shake it off and move on. Step by step, you'll make your way.

for you. They work with these companies to get the lowest interest rate they can, 0 percent, if possible. This doesn't change your monthly payment, but it can change how long you will make payments. Then the credit card accounts will be closed and you'll pay this company, and they'll pay the credit cards. You'll still hear from your credit card companies each month that they received the payment, but your dealings will be with the Debt Management Company.

One other thing: They'll ask you not to add on any credit cards or credit card debts. They'll tell you that you might lose your place in the "program" if you do this. The reason is that the new credit account will show up on your credit report. If one of these companies that have lowered your interest rate sees that you are paying full interest to its competitor, it will raise its interest rates again.

So how do these debt management companies make their money? Through what they call donations. In your amount they may figure in a donation (and they will be up front with you about this and will allow you to decline). For some it's $4 per card they are managing for you. On the other end (if you read the small print, your contract will tell you this), they often receive donations from the credit card companies that come in the form of a percentage of the money they bring in for the company. (This will get paid to a collection agency anyway, so why shouldn't the credit card company donate?)

Put yourself in the shoes of the credit card company. If you've gotten people into a position where they are carrying too much debt, would you rather decrease their interest, or let them fail to pay or declare bankruptcy? Since you, the client, are showing good faith, the credit card company will have a better chance of getting that money this way than letting things get more out of hand for you.

This kind of arrangement does not make the interest tax deductible in any way, but when you think about it. . .since you're paying less interest, you're paying more on your debt and will be out of debt quicker. This is a smart way to approach debt.

Another element that comes into play in working with a debt management company is community and accountability. With that first call you find out that you aren't alone and you aren't the worst-case scenario. There is some comfort in that. You also enter into a relationship in which you are accountable in regard to your debt. Part of the reason our society has gone into debt in such a gargantuan way is that we've felt no consequences, no accountability. Entering into an agreement with a debt management company offers some immediate view to consequences.

Most of these debt management organizations also offer services in regard to foreclosure (if you're about to lose your house or car) and delinquency (if you're so behind on your payments that things have gotten ugly).

First Aid for Your Credit Report

Remember your "permanent record" when you were in school? It was that file you never saw that listed grades and notes and frailties and flaws. There was always a fear of something going onto your permanent record. Why? Because it was permanent; because no matter how much you might have grown up, whoever saw that file would judge you according to your past.

The grown-up version of a permanent record is a credit report. It's not quite as permanent as the file in the principal's office (and possibly not as accurate). It's usually just seven years per black smudge, but it's there for the world to see. Have you seen yours?

You really can order your own credit report, and you might be surprised at what you'll find. There are often mistakes that you will want to correct. Here are the three national bureaus for credit reporting:

❀ TRW (800-392-1122)

❀ TransUnion (800-685-1111)

❀ Equifax (800-916-8800)

You can also go www.myfico.com and for a nominal fee of $12.95, get a copy of your credit report and credit score along with an explanation of what the score means.

With the rise in debt has come the rise of more opportunities for black smudges on your credit report and, thus, more companies that will help you "clean up" your credit report. Be careful whom you trust in this regard. There is something terribly wrong if someone can go into your credit report and change anything there that is the truth. Be careful before believing that this is possible. Be careful even hoping it is. The truth is that while bad credit follows you, it's not the end of the world to live with your own mistakes.

Credit reports keep track of a lot of things, including late payments—thirty days late, sixty days late, and ninety days late. Credit reports will also show bankruptcies and foreclosures. If there is inaccurate information on your credit report, you can change it yourself, but it will take time and consistency and some letter writing.

Loans

Bottom Line

We borrow money for a variety of reasons. The bottom line for every loan, though, is that people want or need something that they don't have the money to buy. Because of this, they borrow the money. We can borrow money from friends, from family, from banks, from vendors, from retail stores, and from car dealerships. It seems like most of the business world is willing and has a structure to help us buy something we don't have the money for.

With loans usually come interest rates. Lenders have been charging interest on loans since the days of Moses in the Old Testament. The Bible has a lot to say about interest rates, in fact. You might have heard the word "usury." It's a word that describes the practice of charging over-the-top interest rates. (God says, "Don't do it." Tell that to your credit card company.)

So loans go back quite a long way and are still going strong. The truth is that seldom do we really *have* to borrow money, but in our culture, waiting and saving are not popular concepts, so most people *do* borrow money from somebody along the way. If you are going to owe someone, be smart about it. Get a good interest rate and borrow as little as possible.

Home Equity

The equity you have in your home is the difference between what you owe on your home and what you could sell it for. If you still owe $60,000 but you could sell it for $70,000, then you have $10,000 equity in your home. Equity in your home is a good thing.

One thing you can do with the equity you have in your home is borrow money against it. You can either get a home equity loan or a home equity line of credit. A home equity loan comes in the form of a lump sum. A home equity line of credit is money that is available to you like the credit limit on a credit card. Home equity loans are what we used to call "second mortgages."

One of the reasons that home equity loans are so popular is that in most cases the interest you pay on the loan or line of credit is tax deductible.

Here are some important points to keep in mind if you are considering borrowing money against the equity in your home.

1. Don't use up all your equity.

Home equity loans have become very popular for loan consolidation. When people get too much debt on credit cards, they can consolidate that debt in a home equity loan and then the interest is tax deductible. It's a great plan, but the downfall is that you then have no equity in your home. There are even 125 percent loans that will let you borrow *more* than the equity that you have in your home. That means that if you need to sell your home, you will owe more to your lenders than you will get for your home. That's a tough place to be.

2. Don't borrow more than $100,000.

If you borrow more than this amount, your interest may not be tax deductible unless you can prove that the money was used for home improvements or business expenses.

3. Home equity loans have become popular loans for college education expenses.

Be careful about this. A home equity loan might be the most conveniently accessible money, but it's not always the cheapest money. Explore all your options before you use up the equity in your home.

Interest Rates

An interest rate is a percentage. That's the simple truth. But while interest rates are simple percentages, there are a lot of ways to apply those rates. It's up to you to read the fine print and know not only your interest rate but also how it is used.

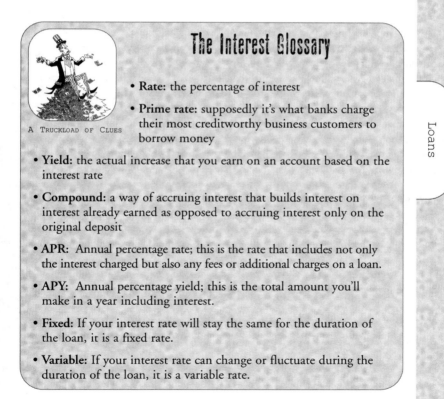

The Interest Glossary

A TRUCKLOAD OF CLUES

- **Rate:** the percentage of interest

- **Prime rate:** supposedly it's what banks charge their most creditworthy business customers to borrow money

- **Yield:** the actual increase that you earn on an account based on the interest rate

- **Compound:** a way of accruing interest that builds interest on interest already earned as opposed to accruing interest only on the original deposit

- **APR:** Annual percentage rate; this is the rate that includes not only the interest charged but also any fees or additional charges on a loan.

- **APY:** Annual percentage yield; this is the total amount you'll make in a year including interest.

- **Fixed:** If your interest rate will stay the same for the duration of the loan, it is a fixed rate.

- **Variable:** If your interest rate can change or fluctuate during the duration of the loan, it is a variable rate.

Loans

Interest rates apply to both money you borrow and interest you earn. The first step to understanding your interest rate is to know what the basic rate is on the account you are opening (or loan you are applying for). When you open a basic savings account you will be quoted an interest rate that is usually between 1 to 2 percent. (That's not very much interest to earn on your money.)

Then, once you know the rate of the interest, you need to figure out what *kind* of interest you'll be earning (or paying). The answer is usually either "simple" interest or "compound" interest. Simple interest is a percentage paid on your original investment. If you put $100 into savings at 10 percent (to keep it easy math), then at the end of the year you will have $110.

Compound interest, on the other hand, pays interest on your original investment, and *then* it pays interest on the interest you have earned. Interest can be compounded every day, month, quarter, or year. (There are a few more ways, but let's keep it uncomplicated for now.) If your interest is compounded monthly, then each month your interest is figured not only on your original deposit but also on the interest you've already earned. The more you have in the account, the more compound interest works for you.

Compound interest is also the way that credit cards make a lot of money off of you. Those balances that you let ride are not only being charged simple interest, they are also being charged compound interest. You are not only paying interest on the money you have on your credit card. You are being charged interest on the interest that you are paying. It's a dirty little game, and when it comes to paying compound interest rather than earning it, you are the loser.

Banks base their interest rates on a lot of different numbers. Sometimes they look at the Federal Reserve's rate for what it charges banks or the rate for what banks charge to borrow money from each other. Other times they raise or lower their prime rate according to the margin that the Federal Reserve raises or lowers its own rates.

Another way that banks apply interest differently is in terms of fixed rates or variable rates. If a loan or account has a fixed rate, then that interest rate stays the same no matter what. On the other hand, if the rate is variable, it can change according to a lot of different measures or indexes. It might rise and fall with the prime rate. It might adjust at scheduled times like an adjustable-rate mortgage.

Interest rates are not always negotiable, and they are not always predictable, but at the opening of a loan or account you should be given some guidelines for how the interest will work on that account. Here are some good questions to ask:

❀ What is the annual percentage yield? This means, "At the end of one year, what will this account be worth?" (If you get them to talk in actual dollars rather than percentages, you can more easily compare accounts.)

❀ Is the interest rate tied to an index? Which one? How often should I expect that index to change?

❀ Is there a limit on how many percentage points my rate can change based on this index?

❀ How often will my interest be compounded?

Car Loans

Unless you have the cash to buy a car, you are going to need to take out a loan of some kind. For most people, that means they will need to borrow money from either a bank, a credit union, or a dealership. Surprisingly, it's often better to shop for your financing before you shop for your car. If you do, not only will you make a smarter purchase, you'll also have a better idea of how much money you can afford to spend. Remember that you may buy a car for $18,000, but once you pay that money out over five years you may have spent over $22,000. Understand your total cost before walking *onto* the lot, not after walking off of it.

Traditionally, haggling has been a big part of car purchases. Car salesmen are notorious for exaggeration and manipulation. If you hate to haggle or you get tired of walking away wondering if you've been suckered, consider going to a no-haggle dealership. Saturn may have been the first, but it isn't the only one anymore.

Once you know how you can best finance your purchase and you're ready to head to the lot, keep these points in mind:

❀ *The best time to buy is at the end of a model year.*
As the year ends, the dealer will want to get rid of that year's model to make room for next year's. This is a good time for you to shop.

❀ *Do your homework on the value of your car.*
If you have a car to trade, take it to a couple of used car dealerships for a bid. This will give you an idea of what a dealership may offer. (Also, ask your local librarian about the resources available to you there for pricing used cars.)

❀ *Don't jump at extended warranties.*
Consider taking the money you would spend on an extended warranty and putting that money in the bank as your own emergency fund for repairs. Why should your money be working for the dealership rather than for you?

❀ *Remember that you don't have to pay sticker price.*
The sticker is the piece of paper on the window that tells what extras the car has, what the gas mileage is, and the suggested price. The sticker

PERSPECTIVE

Leasing or Buying?

Drivers who plan on keeping the same car for five years or more usually come out ahead by buying a car. But if you drive less than 10,000 miles a year, use your car for business, or like to trade every few years, you might be a good candidate for a lease.

Leases look great because they boast lower monthly payments and not much, if any, down payment. But if it sounds too good to be true. . .keep asking questions. Before you sign on a lease you will agree to the monthly cost as well as a payoff at the end of the lease. If your dealer starts talking about "capitalized cost" and "residual cost," slow down and follow closely. Make sure you understand the conditions of the cost at the end of the lease.

Here are some tips to keep in mind:

- While it's better to buy a car late in the year, it's better to lease early in the year.

- Ask about factory-subsidized leases.

- Ask your dealership to lower any up-front costs (down payment, security deposit, etc.).

- Just as with a loan, get the shortest lease possible.

price is not what the dealer paid for it, and it shouldn't be what you pay for it. Most salesmen can easily come down $1,000 from that price.

❀ *Try to put 20 percent down on your new car.*

Not only will that often get you better terms for financing, it will keep your car from losing its value so quickly. The average new car loses more than 40 percent of its value over five years. The more you pay up front, the more you are likely to come out ahead when it's time to trade in.

❀ *Consider using a car-buying service.*

You've probably heard ads on the radio for businesses that car shop for you. You tell them what kind of car you are looking for and they find it. There is a fee involved, but often it's shared by the dealership if not paid by the dealership. Chances are you'll save far more than the fee you will pay. The frustration you'll save will probably outweigh the fee, as well.

When to Rent, When to Buy

Buy? Rent?

One of the greatest joys in life is to be able to go home after a long day at work and prop your feet up on the couch and look around and think, *Yes, this is my place.* There is no greater tangible satisfaction than the knowledge that you have earned enough to provide a home for yourself, a place to hang your hat at the end of the day. While it's great to have your own pad, there are a few factors involved in acquiring a place of residence. A big question to ponder is whether you should rent or buy.

Owning Your Own Home

Owning your own home has many benefits: You can build up equity in your property, and when housing prices rise, you have the option of selling at a profit (if you want to). These benefits are great if you are in a position to pay for them, but don't forget that you have to add on mortgage payments, insurance, property taxes, upkeep, and maintenance fees.

Renting Your Own Home

Here are a few benefits to renting a home:

1. You get more for your money.

2. You're freer to move.

3. You worry less about property values.

4. You can avoid spending.

5. You might have more money to spend in other places.

6. If you don't see yourself staying in your house for a few years, you should probably rent.

7. You find a great deal on the rent.

8. You won't always get a tax break for purchasing a home.

Renting does have a few perks, but the arguments in defense of owning a home are hard to ignore. Federal tax rules favor homeowners. The interest gained from mortgaging your home along with property-tax deductions establish amazing benefits. You can also borrow against the equity of your home (home equity loan) through a second mortgage or a home equity line of credit. Buying a home also gives you "leverage." Because most people purchase their home with a little of their money and lots of someone else's (i.e., the mortgage), using the borrowed money allows you to profit from price increases on property that you haven't even paid for yet.

Consider This

Our lives change so much when we're in the twenties and thirties that buying a home is not always smart at that time.

PERSPECTIVE

Own or Rent?

Here's a quick quiz to help you figure out whether to rent or to buy:

1. What do you consider more important: the quality of your neighborhood or your house?

    a.) Neighborhood

    b.) House

2. If your company offered you a chance to relocate with an immediate pay raise or to stay put with the same pay raise for the next year, how would you respond?

In My Father's Home

HELP FROM ABOVE

God cares about your decisions. The Bible says: "There are many rooms in my Father's home, and I am going to prepare a place for you. If this were not so, I would tell you plainly. When everything is ready, I will come and get you, so that you will always be with me where I am. And you know where I am going and how to get there" (John 14:2–4 NLT).

a.) I'm ready!

b.) No way, I'm stayin' here.

3. Do you try to save a portion of your paycheck?

a.) No

b.) Yes

4. Have you changed jobs more than once in the last three years?

a.) Oui

b.) Non

5. Have you moved more than once in the last three years?

a.) Si

b.) No

If you got more a's than b's, renting is probably the best option for you at this point. Likewise, if you scored mostly b's, call your real estate agent, because you're ready to buy, baby!

Here are some other issues to keep in mind when deciding whether to rent or own a home:

1. Do you have a steady job history?

2. Do you have an established and favorable credit profile?

3. Have you saved the money for a down payment and closing costs?

4. Can you afford the monthly mortgage payments for the house you want?

If you answered "yes" to at least two of the questions, owning a home is definitely a possibility. If not, perhaps renting is the best option for you at this point.

Pros and Cons of Owning a Home

Pros	Cons
Pride of ownership	Responsibilities for maintenance
Having a mortgage may help to discipline your spending	Risk of putting a lot of your financial savings into your "residential basket"
Can remodel and redecorate without the permission of the landlord	Aren't as free to move about

Home Is Where the Heart Is

If you decide to invest in a place to call your own, there are a few neat things to keep in mind!

❀ Because of inflation, you will pay the same amount with even "cheaper dollars" than when you rent.

❀ Your home's value will increase over time.

❀ By owning a home, you become eligible for significant tax advantages that are not available to renters. Owning a home is a serious financial investment. Here are four financial factors that you should calculate when pondering whether or not to purchase:

1. Rental value

2. Appreciation net of depreciation

3. Carrying cost

4. Transaction costs

Mortgages and More

So you want to buy a house. Big decision, isn't it? Unfortunately, even bigger than that decision is the amount of moolah you need to scrape together for a down payment. And that's not the last of it. The more bewildering part is how you're going to get the rest of the money: the mortgage. But what kind of mortgage? How long should the term be? What about all that interest stuff? The mortgage experts here at *Indispensable Guides* have put our heads together, battling the odds (and other numerical expressions), to bring you a clue about the wide world of mortgage loans.

THE BOTTOM LINE

How Big?

You can afford a house that costs between two and three times your annual salary.

Your Wildest Dreams

Unfortunately, it's necessary to keep your feet planted on terra firma when contemplating the purchase of a house. Those things are expensive suckers, and lending institutions have several qualifying guidelines to determine whether you can really afford that cute Cape Cod and whether you'll be able to pay your monthly mortgage payments.

Housing expense ratio

Your total monthly expenses (including mortgage payments, property taxes, and insurance) should be no more than 28 percent of your monthly gross (before-tax) income.

Total debt-to-income ratio

Your total monthly housing expenses plus other long-term debts should be no more than 36 percent of your monthly gross income.

In English

Spend about one-fourth of your income on housing and about one-third on indebtedness, and you'll be able to pay your mortgage with no problem.

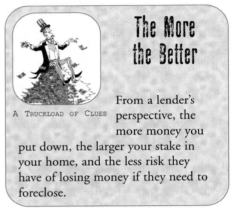

A Truckload of Clues

The More the Better

From a lender's perspective, the more money you put down, the larger your stake in your home, and the less risk they have of losing money if they need to foreclose.

The general rule of thumb is to be able to put down 20 percent of the cost of the house. However, it is possible to get a mortgage with as little as 5 percent down, although this wouldn't be recommended.

Three C's

Besides checking out your ratios, loan institutions also look at a few other goodies, known as the "Three Cs":

Capacity: income, debts, housing expense

Collateral: appraisal, down payment

Credit: payment history

Usually, you need good scores in two of these areas if you want to get that mortgage.

The Makings of a Mortgage Loan

So what happens when you get a mortgage? Basically, the lending institution takes the title to your property as collateral for your repaying the loan, plus a little bonus called *interest*.

The mortgage itself is the amount of money you're borrowing. The term is the number of years you will take to repay that loan. The more cash you put down, the smaller your loan, and therefore the smaller your mortgage payments. The longer the repayment period, the greater amount of interest you'll end up paying.

Types of Mortgage Loans

There are many different types of mortgage loans, so be sure to check them all out before you decide on one kind. You'll probably be able to find one that is most suited to you and your situation. We'll try to enlighten you here.

There are a couple factors to consider in determining what kind of loan you would prefer. A major consideration is how long you're planning on staying in your house. Years? Decades? 'Til it begins to crumble around you?

Fixed-Rate Mortgage Loans

These loans could be renamed "Old Faithful." Once you determine the length of the loan and lock in the interest rate, there isn't too much brain work left than to write the monthly check twelve times a year. This is a good choice if you expect to stay in your abode for a long time.

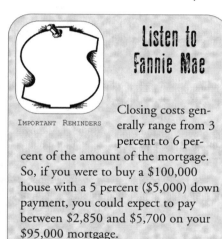

Listen to Fannie Mae

IMPORTANT REMINDERS

Closing costs generally range from 3 percent to 6 percent of the amount of the mortgage. So, if you were to buy a $100,000 house with a 5 percent ($5,000) down payment, you could expect to pay between $2,850 and $5,700 on your $95,000 mortgage.

—FannieMae.com

Pros
❋ There's no risk that your payments will increase.

❋ It's easier to budget.

Cons
❋ It has a high interest rate: It's what you get for security.

❋ It's harder to qualify for: Your payments are higher (in general), and therefore you are a greater risk to the lending organization.

Thirty-Year Fixed-Rate Mortgage Loan
❋ It helps keep your housing expenses low since you're making lots of small payments over a long period of time.

❋ It provides maximum interest deduction for tax purposes.

Twenty-Year Fixed-Rate Mortgage Loan
❋ It often has a lower interest rate than the thirty-year loan.

❋ It amortizes principal and interest over a period of time ten years less than the thirty-year, therefore saving you a bunch of interest.

Fifteen-Year Fixed-Rate Mortgage Loan

❋ A lower interest rate, saving you a lot of interest over the long haul.

❋ It allows you to build up equity in your home more quickly, because you're paying off your mortgage faster.

❋ It's a good choice if you anticipate greater expenses in the future, such as college education, or are anticipating retirement.

❋ The monthly payments are more hefty.

Adjustable-Rate Loans

These loans could be renamed "roller-coaster loans," 'cause you'd better buckle up for this ride (keeping hands, arms, loose clothing, and small house pets clear, please). There are many different kinds of adjustable-rate mortgages (ARM), but the gist of it is that for a specified amount of time (six months to ten years), the interest rate may be relatively low (and therefore a lower monthly payment). After that period, however, your interest rate (payment) is free to adjust to the whims of the financial world, meaning it could go rocketing up or plummeting down. Yep, better hold on.

When talking about adjustable-rate loans, you'll probably hear something about caps. Now, these aren't pen caps, or your favorite team's baseball caps, either. These are *financial* caps, and there are two of them: One limits how high the interest rate can go up, and the other sets the maximum amount of adjustments that can be made over the life of the loan. Now, on to the pros and cons. . .

Pros

❋ The monthly payments on an ARM start out lower than those for fixed-rate. . .and you could qualify for a larger loan.

❋ You're confident your income is going to increase in the future, and you'll be able to handle any increase in payments.

A TRUCKLOAD OF CLUES

Maintenance

Budget 1 percent of the purchase price of your house to cover regular maintenance and unexpected repairs.

❋ You plan on moving within a few years and therefore don't care if the interest rate rises.

Cons

❋ Your interest rate might go up (. . .we told you).

CD-Indexed ARMs (Certificate of Deposit)
❀ After an initial period of six months, the rate and payments adjust every six months, with a per-adjustment cap of 1 percent and a lifetime rate cap of 6 percent.

Treasury-Indexed ARMs
❀ Six-month, one-year, or three-year maturities

❀ The interest rate will adjust every six months, one year, or three years, depending on which security index schedule you are on.

Cost of Funds-Indexed ARMs
❀ Indexed to the actual costs that a certain group of institutions pays to borrow money, such as the Eleventh Federal Home Loan Bank District.

❀ Adjusts every month, every six months, or every year

Initial Fixed-Period ARMs
❀ Doesn't adjust interest rate until several years after you take out the loan, offering several years of fixed payments until then.

❀ Three-, five-, seven-, or ten-year fixed-period ARMs are available.

Thirty-Year Loan Example
❀ 10/1 ARM: Has a fixed interest rate and monthly payments for the first ten years and then an annually adjustable interest rate for the remaining twenty years.

❀ 7/1: Has a fixed interest rate and monthly payments for the first seven years and then an annually adjustable interest rate for the remaining twenty-three years.

You get the picture and can probably do the math for the 5/1 and 3/1; the one-year ARM adjusts annually, and the six-month ARM does so every six months.

Balloon Mortgages
There is no better name for these mortgages: They start out pretty flat and limp, but before you know it, they're flying high above you. After the first five or seven years of low interest rates, all of a sudden you have to repay the entire loan balance or drastically refinance!

Pros
❀ Have lower interest rates, which are good for shorter-term financing.

❀ It's easier to qualify (because it is a very short loan).

❋ You have protection from rate increases.

❋ They are great if you're only planning to live in your home a few years.

Cons

❋ You're forced to refinance or sell in five or seven years.

❋ If you refinance, the interest rate might be higher.

Piggy Bank

IMPORTANT REMINDERS

In many cases, your lender will want you to have two months' of mortgage payments saved up as a cash reserve when you apply for your mortgage.

Government Loans

There are a number of government loans that are especially helpful for low- to moderate-income folks, and those that are buying a home for the first time.

FHA Loans

You can purchase a home with a down payment as low as 3 to 5 percent of the appraisal value or the purchase price, whichever is lower.

VA Loans

This is the good one. A qualified veteran can buy a house costing up to $203,000. . . with no down payment! In addition, the qualification guidelines for VA loans are more flexible than other loans.

State and Local Loan Programs

Knowing the enormity of trying to get enough cash together for that down payment, many states have programs to help first-time home buyers qualify for a mortgage. They offer either a low down payment or low interest rate to buyers who meet specified income guidelines.

Whatever You Do. . .

Have fun! This is a very exciting time in your life, and with a little careful thought and research, buying a home won't be nearly as draining as trying to scrape six layers of stubborn wallpaper off the walls of your new dining room.

Taxes

Tax Man

With lyrics like those in "Taxman," George Harrison and the Beatles were almost guaranteed an instant hit from the first time their pens touched the paper, regardless of cultural orientation. Getting people to identify with a sense of resentment toward their respective tax collection agencies is still quite comparable to shooting fish in a barrel.

Don't agree? Try and read the next few words without a shudder: Tax day. The IRS. Uncle Penny-Pincher. Blood from a stone. To most of us, these ideas are all associated in one way or another, all filed in the deep, dark, "only-think-about-when-absolutely-necessary" section of our mental catalog.

With the exception of those who choose to run their own counterfeiting business out of the basement, perhaps, all of us feel the sting of taxes. And most of us are reminded of the concept of taxation every payday. You open the envelope. Your eyes dart for the bottom line. Your stomach sinks a little. *Where's the rest?* you wonder. Then you notice that nasty little section with all the minuses before each number. Federal income tax. Social Security tax. Medicare tax. State income tax. Street tax. Seat tax. Heat tax. Perhaps not to the extreme that the Fab Four chose to portray, but the bottom line is that taxes, and the paying of them, are an unavoidable reality.

All those in search of a mystical tax-be-gone formula somewhere within the seven pages of this section can save themselves from prolonged disappointment

Guilty

All of us have probably heard the one about the IRS's Guilt Division, but just in case. . .

AMAZING STORIES AND FACTS

One year Bob P. Taxpayer came down with a bad case of the (conscience-induced) post-tax-day blues. Knowing full well he had been a little less than honest with Uncle Sam in the twenty-plus years he'd been earning taxable income, he was moved by the Spirit to send a reimbursement check to the tune of 7,000 big ones. Included with the check was a letter Bob had written in order to best explain the situation. It read,

Dear Uncle Sam,

Have been having trouble sleeping. This is your money, not mine.

Apologetically,
Robert P. Taxpayer

P.S. If most of the guilt doesn't go away by next Tuesday, I'll send the other $14,000.

by flipping ahead to the next one now. (And that's not to say that you'll find it there, either!)

Although there are a handful of money-saving strategies we've deemed worthy of mention, there is simply no way around the yearly practice of reimbursing the government for the services they provide us. Never thought of it that way?

How would you feel were you to arrive at your place of employment early tomorrow morning only to hear the boss say, "Sorry, Susie. Look, you do great things around here, and we want you to know that we really appreciate your consistent efforts to better our business. The rub is, a few of the other executives and I got together last night and decided not to pay you for the past year of work. In fact, I probably ought to tell you that if you want any money whatsoever, you're going to have to hunt us down and beat it out of us, because we also all agreed to go into hiding for a while until the whole thing just blows over. And, oh, yes, should you want to keep working here, you can. Volunteer work looks real good on a resumé, you know."

Starting to get the picture? The taxes, like the show, must be paid. (Or is it "go on"?) At any rate, if you've successfully convinced yourself of this truth, you now have a few decisions to make.

The Bible and Taxes. . .

HELP FROM ABOVE

Curious as to what the Bible has to say about taxes? Check out these passages:

" 'Tell us then, what is your opinion? Is it right to pay taxes to Caesar or not?' But Jesus, knowing their evil intent, said, 'You hypocrites, why are you trying to trap me? Show me the coin used for paying the tax.' They brought him a denarius, and he asked them, 'Whose portrait is this? And whose inscription?' 'Caesar's,' they replied. Then he said to them, 'Give to Caesar what is Caesar's, and to God what is God's' " (Matthew 22:17–21).

"Give everyone what you owe him: If you owe taxes, pay taxes; if revenue, then revenue; if respect, then respect; if honor, then honor. Let no debt remain outstanding, except the continuing debt to love one another, for he who loves his fellowman has fulfilled the law" (Romans 13:7–8).

"Obey the laws, then, for two reasons: first, to keep from being punished, and second, just because you know you should. Pay your taxes too, for these same two reasons. For government workers need to be paid so that they can keep on doing God's work, serving you" (Romans 13:5–6 TLB).

Take This Quiz...

Filing your own taxes, unlike tying your shoes, has only gotten more and more complex with time. More and more people each year are choosing to forego the late nights with their calculators and Advil bottles and instead hand over the responsibility to qualified professionals. There is no shame in the decision to do so. But if you're feeling up to the task, why not take a few seconds and test your knowledge of current tax code? Go on, Mister Smarty Taxes, grab a pencil and see if you're still up to snuff!

1. Which would you rather have?

    a.) A credit of $100

    b.) A cool $100 in your pocket

    c.) 101 Dalmatians

    d.) A deductible expense of $100

2. All of the following are typically considered "income" except:

    a.) A $200 Christmas bonus

    b.) Alimony of $100

    c.) A $900 unemployment check

    d.) Social Security payments of $100

3. All of the following are normally deductible except:

    a.) Home equity interest on principal borrowed in excess of $100,000

    b.) Calls to Stinky Pete, your investment broker

    c.) A subscription to the Microsoft Network for investment purposes

    d.) Business compensation paid to your children under eighteen

4. Which of the following are not deductible as medical expenses?

    a.) The bus fare to the doctor's office

    b.) Whirlpool (not the dishwasher) treatment prescribed for arthritis

    c.) Life insurance

    d.) Swim club dues (when a physician has prescribed swimming to alleviate a medical condition)

5. Which of the following is normally not deductible?

a.) Giving your dad's old moth-ridden leisure suit to charity

b.) Credit card interest

c.) Job-hunting expenses

d.) Tax-planning advice from a non-accountant

ANSWERS—1a; 2d; 3a; 4c; 5b

Dealing with the Forms

How'd you do? Starting to reconsider? Perhaps you're still confident of your abilities? In that case, it's time to get started.

Tax strategists agree, although the road toward completing your own tax return can be a hard one, it certainly need not be impossible. The fine folks at moneycentral.msn.com offer the following four-step program:

A TRUCKLOAD OF CLUES

Tax Help Online?

Having trouble with your taxes (again)? Pleading ignorance won't help, so why not check out a few of the countless, friendly, tax-related sites on the Net?

www.irs.gov
www.irs.ustreas.gov
www.unclefed.com
www.armchairmillionaire.com/tax
www.taxwizard.com
www.taxcut.com
www.turbotax.com
www.e1040.com

www.taxanalysts.com
www.taxhelponline.com
www.taxworld.org
www.taxprophet.com
www.irs.com
www.tax.org
www.handrblock.com

Remember—the Web is an ever-changing storehouse of information. To stay on top of things, it probably wouldn't hurt to run a search of your own. (Try "help with taxes," "tax help," etc.)

Taxes

1. Get organized and get started.

Tax planning, contrary to popular opinion, is not what you do on April 14th. Smart tax planning is a year-round process.

2. Understand the basics.

A simple understanding of a few key strategies can save you big bucks come tax time. It's also not a bad idea to look into using your computer to prepare your taxes. The IRS notes an error rate of 20 percent over recent years; comparable to an error rate near 1 percent on returns filed electronically. PC tax preparation is easy and accurate. What takes you hours to prepare manually may only be a click away on the computer.

THE BOTTOM LINE

Form 1040EZ

Form 1040EZ is undoubtedly the easiest of all possible tax return forms, especially when trying to file your own taxes. If you're wondering whether you qualify, take a deep breath and see how well you match up against the following criteria:

Your filing status is single or married filing jointly. You (and your spouse, if married filing a joint return) are not sixty-five or older or blind. You do not claim any dependents. Your taxable income is less than $50,000. Your income is only from wages, salaries, tips, unemployment compensation, taxable scholarship and fellowship grants, and taxable interest of $400 or less. You did not receive any advance earned-income credit payments. If you are married filing jointly and either you or your spouse worked for more than one employer, the total wages of that person were not over $62,700. You do not itemize deductions, claim any adjustments to your income or tax credits other than the earned-income credit, or owe any taxes other than the amount from the tax table. If you do not meet any one of these requirements, you must use Form 1040A or Form 1040. And if you just read all of that in one sitting, go have a sundae. You deserve a reward.

3. Remember to maximize your deductions and credits.

This has a lot to do with how well you've done your research: It's also one of the most effective ways you can lower your tax bill.

Don't Forget

IMPORTANT REMINDERS

. . .Obviously, to pay your taxes, and on time! Tax day is April 15. (Don't say you weren't warned, either: There is a penalty for late filing of 5 percent of the tax not paid by the due date for each month or part of a month your return is late!)

You can reach the IRS by dialing 1-800-TAX-1040 (when trying to resolve a problem that has thus far seen no resolution through usual IRS channels, contact the Problem Resolution Programs office at 1-877-777-4778).

File copies of your W-2 form(s) appropriately: one with your federal tax return and one with your state income tax return. It's a good idea to hold on to at least one other copy as well, for your own records.

Not being able to pay your taxes come April 15th is not an instant, one-way ticket to the slammer. Such a plight is far from unusual. Mail your return on time, regardless of your ability (or lack thereof) to pay it. You do have the option to pursue payment in monthly installments (look into Form 9465). If approved, you will be charged a $43 fee; but don't submit the fee with your form, as it is usually deducted from your first payment after the approval of your request.

4. Compare your results.

Check your answers against MSN's "Tax Estimator" by clicking onto the aforementioned Web site.

Should you choose to prepare your own taxes, may the force be with you, as they say. Remember—although how you choose to pay them is up to you, paying them is inevitable, a biblical mandate, and a nice way to keep yourself out of jail.

Taxes

Cutting the Tax Bill

Jeff Schnepper, tax attorney and author of the book *How to Pay Zero Taxes*, offers five key strategies to cut the tax bill:

1. Minimize Your Gross Income

Converting taxable income into nontaxable income is an automatic tax reduction. There are a number of ways Joe P. Taxpayer can go about doing this, the simplest of which being the decision to invest in tax-free (rather than taxable) investments.

Modifying your compensation arrangement with your employer is another step in the right direction. (For example, asking your employer to help pay your college tuition in lieu of a bonus; giving up earned income in exchange for alternatives such as accident and health plans, hospitalization and group life insurance premiums, participation in qualified retirement plans, and other such forms of nontaxable compensation, etc.)

2. Turn Everyday Expenditures into Deductions

Some personal expenses can be deducted as business expenses. (Some, not all. This involves a personal, ethical judgment call.) For example, if you work out of a home office, you may be able to deduct some furniture and equipment (such as a computer or fax machine), a portion of your home insurance, mortgage interest, real estate taxes, heating, air-conditioning, and even depreciation on part of the house.

If you're a small-business owner with children capable of working for you, keep it in the bloodline! If your kids can work for you, you are converting their personal allowance into deductible compensation. Furthermore, if your kids are under eighteen and work for your (unincorporated) business, Social Security and Medicare taxes need not be paid.

3. Use Your Special Tax Credits

Take advantage of special credits allowed for by the tax code. And remember to be on the lookout for new ones, as well. These can really pay off: For example, a $100 tax credit reduces your tax by $100, whereas a $100 deduction (in the 31 percent bracket) reduces your tax by only $31.

4. Know Your Marginal Rate

If you're like most of the people thumbing through this chapter, you're probably wondering what a marginal rate is, let alone *your* marginal rate. Be unafraid, for you are not alone! Your marginal rate is the rate of tax you pay on your next dollar of taxable income. (The higher your taxable income, the higher your marginal rate.) It is possible to reduce your tax by allocating income to different family members in lower tax brackets. For example, shifting $10,000 in mutual funds earning 10 percent into your son's name is the equivalent of shifting $1,000 in income from your bracket to his. (Bear in mind that although this is saving you tax dollars, the $10,000 now belongs to your son. How much do you love Junior, in other words?)

5. Take Advantage of All Your Deductions

With a Congress-created tax code full of deductions (some call them "loopholes") serving a variety of purposes, it only makes sense to take advantage of them. Not doing so is the same as making an involuntary contribution to the IRS (which, for the record, is foolish—voluntary contributions to the government are deductible). To modify the wisdom of GI Joe, knowing is, in this instance, more than half the battle. Knowing your deductions can pay off: Cutting $1,000 off your tax bill each year and investing that money in an IRA account adds up to about $40,000 after twenty years and $90,000 after thirty (yikes!).

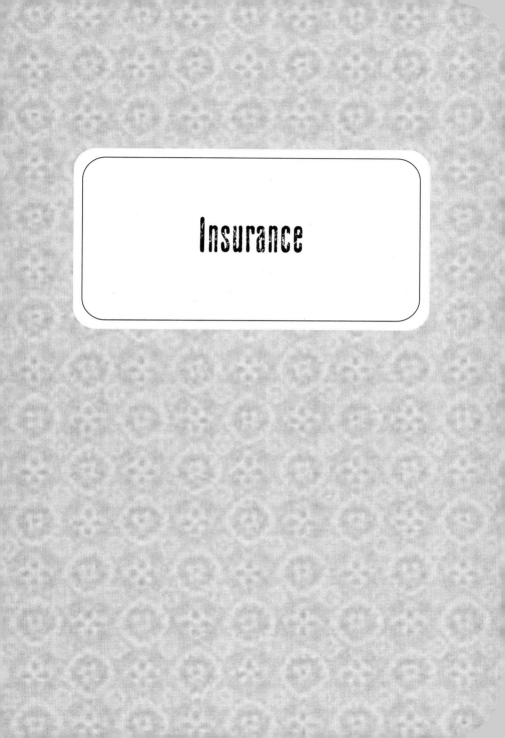

Insurance

Limiting Risk

Insurance is all about limiting risk. While the insurance market that we recognize today began with Lloyd's of London, people have been finding ways to limit risk throughout civilization. The first insurers covered shipping losses. Next came losses by fire. In America, the first fire insurance company was formed by Benjamin Franklin. Since then, the act of insuring losses and limiting risks has become a monster of an industry. In fact, according to Ralph Nader and Wesley Smith, the premiums paid for insurance (of all kinds) in America in 1990 was three times the national budget deficit.

Basically, this is how it works. People "buy" insurance from companies. They sign an agreement or contract, and they pay a premium or payment. The agreement is based on several factors:

1. The probability that a loss will occur

2. The potential size of the loss

3. The percentage of the potential loss that the company will pay

The buyers all pay their premiums and hope for the best. When a loss does occur, the company pays what they have agreed to pay (hopefully without too much fuss and bother) out of the money they have made from all the premiums. So everybody is funding everybody else's losses. At the end of the year, whatever the company has not had to pay out against the losses is theirs as profit. It's all a guessing game—sort of a gamble. Buyers pay a fixed amount so that they won't have to face a catastrophe. If they don't come up against a catastrophe, then they've paid their fixed amount just for the peace of mind.

Life

Talking about life insurance can be a little bit morbid, but these days, it is a necessary evil. And, in reality, it functions as:

An investment

Many forms of life insurance act as investments in which you earn cash and portions of your premiums earn money. Some also provide income after you reach a certain age.

A tax shelter

Often when money accrues in a life insurance policy, it is tax-deferred. That means you won't be taxed on it until you withdraw it. If the proceeds are withdrawn by your family upon your death, they are still not taxable. This means your money works harder for you while you are alive and harder for your family after you are gone.

A TRUCKLOAD OF CLUES

An Insurance Glossary

- **Premium:** The payments that you make to your insurance company in trade for the policy

- **Policy:** The contract or agreement that you have made with your insurance company

- **Loss:** When we lose anything that is of benefit to us whether it is a possession or a condition (such as our health)

- **Risk:** The likelihood that we will experience a loss

- **Deductible:** The part of the loss that the insured must pay. Often, the higher the premium that you pay the less your deductible is.

- **Personal insurance:** Insurance that protects individuals and families

- **Commercial insurance:** Insurance that protects companies or businesses

- **Agent:** An independent agent is a person who represents different insurance companies at the same time and works for a percentage of your premiums. An exclusive agent is a person that sells insurance for only one company and probably works on commission from that company.

- **Broker:** An agent represents a company or several companies. A broker represents the buyer (you) and shops around at many companies to find the best price and policy.

A way to support your beneficiaries
The money that your life insurance policy guarantees your beneficiaries gives you a way to provide for them as they deal with losing you.

An estate-planning tool
If set up properly, your life insurance policy can help you avoid estate taxes. There are several types of life insurance policies.

    1. Term Insurance. This is the plain-Jane-nothing-fancy policy. It covers you for a specific time frame (the term), and the basic agreement is that if you die during the term, the agreed-upon amount of money will be paid to your beneficiaries. No money accrues, and there is no reimbursement of the premiums once the term is up.

The Anatomy of an Insurance Policy

- **The declarations page:** There are the vital stats. It's the cars covered, the address of the house, the name of the company, the effective date, the type of policy, the extent of the coverage, your representative's signature. This might be the only part of the policy that is customized to your information.

- **Definitions section:** This section explains whom the policy is about and in regard to. Any people affected by the policy should be defined here.

- **The agreement:** This is the heart of the policy. It tells the exact terms of the contract. The agreement is often broken down into sections that define the policy.

- **Exclusions:** Exactly what areas of loss are not covered or protected by the contract.

- **Conditions:** Your obligations under the policy and your duties after the loss occurs.

- **Endorsements and riders:** If you fill in any gaps or make any changes to the standard policy, they will be listed here.

2. Cash Value Policies. With these policies, your money is invested and cash is accrued. You can use this cash in several ways. You can cancel the policy and use the cash or reinvest it. You can also borrow against the policy, using it as collateral.

3. Annuities. Annuities actually pay out money to the insured and, if agreed upon in the contract, to the beneficiaries. Many people use this kind of life insurance as a retirement fund.

No matter what type of life insurance policy you are dealing with, there are three people involved. First, there is the owner. This is the person who bought the policy. It may or may not be the person who is insured. For instance, if a parent takes life insurance out on his children, the children are the insured, but the parent is the owner of the policy. The owner has the right to name the beneficiaries, to make decisions about how the cash is used, and to make changes to the policies and how the benefits of the policy will be settled.

There can be a lot of confusion about who owns an insurance policy. Often the person who is insured may assume that he has the right to make decisions about the policy or to cash it out. But unless the insured is the owner, he can't make any of those kinds of decisions.

Once the insured has passed away, there are several ways that the benefits of the policy can be settled.

❀ Lump sum. A one-time payment of the total benefits is disbursed.

❀ Interest payments only. An account can be established and the beneficiaries paid the interest earned on the settlement. Sometimes the beneficiaries can choose to withdraw part or all of the principal, as well.

❀ Installment payments. The benefits are paid out over a specific period of time. This is often used if a parent leaves money to children and allots it to them as they reach certain ages.

❀ Life income. In this kind of settlement the beneficiary can't withdraw principal. Instead he or she gets regular periodic payment for a minimum amount of time.

❀ Customized arrangements. If you need to have the money distributed in an unusual manner, go ahead and work it out with your insurance company. They usually have the flexibility to work with you.

There can be exclusions in life insurance policies. Sometimes benefits are modified or withheld in case of suicide, dangerous activities, or war-related activities.

Car

Most states require a driver to have insurance in order to drive his car. Some states are considered no-fault states. This means that when they settle claims, they don't make every decision based on whose fault the accident was. Other states use traditional third-party systems for settling claims. That means courts and blame and who did what. Neither way is perfect or easy.

Most insurance policies will answer these questions:

1. Who Is Covered in the Policy?

These people are called the "insureds." They can include the driver, his family, and anyone he gives permission to drive the car. If the insurance is in relation to a business, this can also include employees.

2. What Type of Coverage?

Your auto insurance policy is actually a collection of different kinds of coverage in varying amounts. You may not realize it, but you have a part in deciding how those kinds of coverage are divided. There are basically three types:

❀ *Liability: coverage for damage*
This is the most expensive and the most controversial part of your coverage. It is designed to protect against the costs of being sued. It addresses bodily injury (including med pay or who gets medical benefits), property damage, and the cost of the lawsuit.

❀ *Collision or comprehensive: coverage for damage to your car*
Usually this is about one-third of the cost of your policy. It protects the value of your car. Collision covers contact between your vehicle and another vehicle or large object. Comprehensive covers loss by mischief, an animal, fire, theft, a storm, or flying objects.

❀ *Uninsured motorists: protection from uninsured or underinsured drivers*
As insurance costs have risen, this part of your insurance has become more and more important. Its purpose is to cover your own bodily injury. It is based on fault. If it was your fault, then you don't receive benefits. This part of your insurance pays what you would have been entitled to if the other driver had had insurance.

3. What Miscellaneous Coverage Do You Want to Buy?

There are some smaller coverage options that you can purchase, such as rental car reimbursement and towing.

Pricing

Several factors will determine the price of your auto insurance.

❀ Where you live. Companies rate the territories in your city based on accident statistics for each area.

❀ Your personal stats. Age (younger drivers have more accidents), gender (young unmarried men have more accidents), marital status (married drivers have fewer accidents).

❀ How you use the car. Do you use it for business? Do you put a lot of miles on the car?

❀ The kind of car. The safer the car, the lower the premiums. On the other hand, the more expensive the repairs, the higher the premiums.

❀ Your driving record. Both accidents and convictions (tickets) are taken into account. The more you have, the higher the premiums.

❀ The extent of your insurance. If you have a lot of coverage, then you will have a high premium. The more risk to the company, the more you'll pay to cover that risk.

Crunch

If you've ever had an automobile accident, then you are probably familiar with at least a few of the steps below. Here are the typical steps of an automobile claims case:

1. The accident happens. Information is exchanged.

2. The accident is investigated. There is usually a police report. The insurance companies do their own evaluation of the facts.

3. Medical treatment is received by both parties if necessary. Doctors send out bills.

4. A settlement is negotiated. Once the consequences of the accident have been tallied as much as is possible, the insurance adjuster will make an attempt to resolve the case. The injured parties may have an attorney involved, but at this point the discussions take place out of court. It can all end here if the parties are agreed.

5. A lawsuit is filed. If the parties are not agreed, then there is usually a lawsuit with defense lawyers on one side and the plaintiff on the other.

6. People are deposed and facts are reviewed. In lawyer-speak this is called *discovery*. The plaintiff (the one complaining) will be thoroughly researched, including medical history. This part of the process can be exhausting and time consuming.

7. A settlement is renegotiated. During the discovery process the lawyers can meet and discuss a way to settle out of court.

8. A trial. If there isn't a settlement yet, then the case goes to court, and the decision is left up to a jury, judge, or arbitrator as to who will be reimbursed and for what and how much.

9. An appeal of the decision. If the decisions don't suit either party, they can appeal the decision. Sometimes the case is retried.

As you can see, there are some elements to the price of your insurance that you have no control over. There are some things you can do, though, to get a better price on insurance.

- ❀ Shop around. Don't assume prices are all the same.

- ❀ Take higher deductibles and keep some money in the bank for emergencies.

- ❀ Keep your driving record clean as a whistle. Buy safe cars.

- ❀ Call your insurance company before you buy to find out how your next car purchase will affect your rates.

- ❀ Refuse some of the options. Pay for your own towing, for instance, rather than paying for coverage whether you ever get towed or not.

- ❀ Ask about discounts. Many companies give discounts for having more than one car with the same insurance agency, or for nonsmokers or driving classes.

- ❀ Find out if your health insurance company handles auto insurance and vice versa.

Health

Heath insurance is a must in today's world. The costs of health care and hospitalization have skyrocketed to the point where one serious illness can wipe out a lifetime of savings.

There are several kinds of health insurance:

Traditional
Traditional health insurance usually includes three categories of coverage. First is hospitalization, which (obviously) covers expenses you incur if you are hospitalized. Second is medical/surgical, which covers everything outside of the hospital, like doctors' visits and treatments. There is usually some kind of deductible or copayment required. Finally there is catastrophic or major medical (makes you take a big gulp just to use a word like "catastrophic," doesn't it?). This kind of insurance covers gaps that are left by the first two categories, as well as the far greater expenses of a major illness or injury that won't be covered by the other two.

HMOs
Traditional health insurance costs more than HMOs and requires more out-of-pocket payments. HMOs cost less and sometimes have no additional out-of-pocket payments. The trade-off is that with an HMO you have substantially less freedom in who will treat you. An HMO (health maintenance organization) is a network of caregivers. The choices are increasing within the network, but if your family physician isn't on the list, you are still out of luck.

PPOs
PPOs are preferred provider organizations. They try to give the best of traditional

insurance and the best of HMOs. They still preselect your choices of care-givers but offer a higher level of care as the trade-off.

Disability

In fact, disability insurance doesn't pay for health care at all. It actually pays for lost wages that result from an injury or illness. It is considered a part of the health care package, though.

You can get health care in a group policy, as an individual policy, or through government benefits. For individual policies, the cost can be quite high, but individual insurance has come a long way with the increase of small business and self-employed people. Group policies have the advantage of higher benefits, lower deductibles, and easy acceptance (often medical exams are not even required). Government benefits include Medicare (for senior citizens and the disabled), Medicaid (for the poor), and the Veterans Administration.

The price of health insurance is based on a combination of factors, including age, the amount of people on the policy, gender (women usually require more coverage), health history, occupation, and lifestyle (smoker? drinker? stressful job?).

Most people are unaware of the costs of health insurance because they have it through their employer or their spouse's employer. It's not until you change jobs or lose coverage that you face the expense of health insurance. If you do change jobs or have a lapse in group coverage, there are several ways you can keep some kind of health insurance coverage available. Through COBRA (Congressional Omnibus Budget Reconciliation Act) benefits, you can often continue your group coverage for eighteen months if you'll pay the total amount. If COBRA benefits aren't available, you can sometimes convert your group policy into an individual policy. If you lose your group coverage altogether, you can purchase a short-term policy, just to tide you over until you figure out a long-term plan. You can also join some professional or trade organizations that include a group policy as a benefit to members. Even credit card companies sometimes offer group memberships.

Homeowner's

Homeowner's insurance is perhaps the most standardized kind of insurance available. It also can be the most cost effective. All insurance policies are a risk for you and for the insurer because the insurer is betting that nothing will happen so they can keep your money. The truth is that people are more careful with their homes than with anything else, so there is less risk for the insurer. Also, homes don't roll down the highway at 60 miles per hour, so there is less danger to contend with. Most homeowner's insurance is divided into these categories:

HO-1

Protects against ten named perils. This is the most basic form of homeowner's insurance but is rarely considered enough coverage these days. Some states don't even offer it anymore. The ten perils are usually some combination of fire/lightning, windstorms/hail, explosions, riot, aircraft crashes, damage caused by vehicles, smoke damage, damage by mischief or vandalism, and volcanic eruption.

HO-2

Protects against sixteen named perils. While this broader coverage costs 5 to 10 percent more than HO-1, it is a more appropriate amount of coverage. The additional coverage includes falling objects, weight of snow, sleet, or ice, water damage, defects in heating and air-conditioning systems, freezing water systems, and electrical malfunctions.

HO-3

Instead of naming the perils you are protected from, this policy names only the ones you are not protected (or excluded) from. It is 10 to 15 percent more expensive than HO-1. Some typical exclusions include collapse of the structure due to faulty construction, freezing when the dwelling is vacant, vandalism if the dwelling has been vacant more than thirty days, general power failure, neglect, earth movement, war, nuclear hazard, and on and on. (It gets pretty depressing to have to see a list of all that *could* happen to your home.)

HO-4

Renter's insurance. This policy protects your contents when you are renting but not the structure you are renting.

HO-5

Doesn't really exist anymore. It's like that thirteenth floor. The number is in the elevator, but it never stops there.

HO-6

This policy works for co-op or condominium owners. It protects their possessions like renter's insurance, but it also protects improvements they have made structurally to their homes.

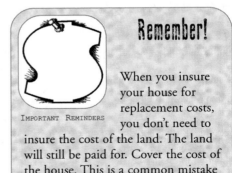

IMPORTANT REMINDERS

Remember!

When you insure your house for replacement costs, you don't need to insure the cost of the land. The land will still be paid for. Cover the cost of the house. This is a common mistake that leaves homeowners overinsured.

HO-8

This is like HO-1, the basics, but it is usually for older homes. Instead of replacement costs, it covers the house for repair costs. That's because replacement costs entail rebuilding a home with the materials and details of the original. With some older homes that would just be impossible and at least cost-prohibitive.

Most homeowners are covered under a policy that would fit into the HO-3 category. As with any other type of insurance, there is additional coverage that you can purchase, and there is a certain amount of customization that you can do to fit your life and needs.

Insurance

Retirement

How Much Will I Need?

It would be great if there were a magic number out there; a percentage based on earnings and multiplied by something or the other that would tell you exactly how much money you will need when you retire. But the truth is that you are the only one who knows what lifestyle you will have upon retirement and what your needs will be based on that lifestyle. So like the Good Witch said to Dorothy, "You've always had the answer within you."

The first place to look to find that answer is your lifestyle right now. What are your monthly budgeted expenses? (You do have a budget, don't you?) Make a list of those expenses, and beside each one list how it will change upon your retirement.

❈ Will you have some of your bills (like mortgages or car loans) paid off?

❈ How will retirement affect your food and transportation bills since you won't be going to work?

❈ Are you hoping to do a lot of traveling?

❈ How much will you be receiving from any pension plans you've paid into?

❈ How much will you be receiving from Social Security?

❈ Will your spouse be making any career changes at the same time that you do?

THE BOTTOM LINE

Get Ready. . .

Grill yourself with these kinds of questions:

• When do I want to retire?

• What kind of lifestyle do I want to have?

• Whom do I want around me when I retire?

• What am I willing to sacrifice now so that I will have more when I retire?

❈ Do you have any health conditions that will be expensive to treat?

❈ Will your health insurance change significantly upon retirement?

Once you know what bills you have now, you can estimate how much money you will need then.

Remember, though, to account for inflation when you think about retirement. Most financial books that you read will state 2 to 4 percent as the yearly rate of inflation. So to really know how much your lifestyle will cost, you have to figure that in. If it costs you $1,000 a month just to keep the household running right now and if inflation is at 4 percent, then next year it will take you ($1,000 X .04 = 40) $1,040 to run that same household. If you continue that equation for as many years as you have until retirement, *then* you'll know how much it will take to run your household.

Household expenses	Yearly inflation increase
Age 55	$1,000.000.04
Age 56	$1,040.000.04
Age 57	$1,081.600.04
Age 58	$1,124.860.04
Age 59	$1,169.860.04
Age 60	$1,216.650.04
Age 61	$1,265.320.04
Age 62	$1,315.930.04
Age 63	$1,368.570.04
Age 64	$1,423.310.04
Age 65	$1,480.240.04
Age 66	$1,539.45 and so on. . .

So if it takes you $1,000 a month to run your household when you are fifty-five, then when you retire at sixty-five, you'll need over $1,500 for the same expenses. That's not even including the traveling you want to do and the new stuff you want to buy and those hobbies that you've been putting off for years.

So, in one way, figuring out how much you need when you retire really is a mathematical equation. It's just not one that people enjoy working through.

When Should I Start Saving for Retirement?

Here's one word for you: now.

Here are two more: compound interest.

And here's a whole sentence: If you save a little now, it will make a *lot* of difference later.

If you're in junior high school (or younger) reading this book then, okay, maybe saving for retirement shouldn't necessarily be at the top of your list of priorities. If you're in high school or college, sure, you probably have other things weighing more heavily on your mind. But if you're out of school and (hopefully) working, retirement should appear on your priority list somewhere, even if it doesn't loom large in the top ten items. Why? Because the younger you are the more a little savings will matter to your retirement. That is the beauty of the two-word answer above: compound interest. Now in regard to your debts, compound interest is a dirty word (four letters or not). It means the credit card companies charge you interest and interest on your interest and interest on the interest that they charged you for. But in regard to a savings fund of some kind, compound interest is one of your greatest friends. It means you save money that earns interest, and then you earn interest on the money *and* interest that you've already earned.

Is that too confusing? Look at it this way. . . .

If Person #1—we'll call him Eric—let's say Eric started at the age of twenty saving $1,000 a year and saved $1,000 per year for ten years. Then let's suppose that Eric foolishly stopped saving *anything. . .at all.* (But in his favor, he didn't take anything out of savings either.) Now let's suppose that Person #2—we'll call him Ian—saved nothing in his twenties but buckled down starting with his thirtieth birthday. Let's say he started saving $1,000 a year and kept on faithfully until he was sixty-five.

It's obvious who made the bigger investment: Ian. He invested $35,000. Eric only invested $10,000. Here's the mind-blowing riddle. Who do you think would have saved more money? Of course, since you're supposed to be amazed at the answer, it must be Eric, and indeed, it is. Eric's ten years of discipline would have outdone Ian's even though he actually invested less than half of Ian's original investment. That's the beauty of compound interest and time. All those years when Eric wasn't saving, the money he had already saved was building, working, growing, and multiplying, like some benevolent virus that would one day cure most of Eric's retirement woes.

Ian? He still did a great job, better than most. But the fact that even with all his work he came in second in this savings game is his legacy to us that the early bird really does get the fattest worm in the saving-for-retirement scenario.

But even if you aren't in your twenties or thirties or even your forties, compound interest is still your friend and even a $25 donation to your own retirement encased in some kind of savings vehicle (like the ones listed on pages 177–182) is money that you have invested in your future.

When should you start saving? Right now.

How Much Do I Need to Start Saving?
How Often Should I Save?

Most financial gurus, if you follow them around long enough and pester them hard enough ("Please tell me, *please*. . .") will eventually suggest that you save 10 percent of each paycheck. (They will then make you sign a paper saying that if for any reason this suggestion backfires they are not liable for life or livelihood. Go ahead and sign—it's a pretty safe bet.)

By saving a percentage rather than a fixed amount, you will naturally increase your savings with your cost of living. By taking it out as you deposit your paycheck you will miss it less. By taking it out of each paycheck you miss smaller bits.

This is the big facade of savings. A little bit just looks like a little bit, but it's really not. It's really a part of a much bigger bit. When you're sitting there with the little bit you think, *What difference will this make? I can use this little bit for something I need right now. Savings is so long-term. Savings won't miss my little bit.*

There's your mistake right there. What will actually happen is that you will spend your little bit on something short term and it will be gone, vanished. But, in the alternate reality, if you let that little bit stay in incubation, it will grow and grow and become its own entity, an entity that you will not recognize as its little-bit former self. An entity that won't take over the world but will be at your beck and call when you really need it, like when you need it to support you after you retire.

Don't let the savings facade confuse you. Keep making the sacrifice of that little bit. You might miss out on a trip to Dairy Queen today, but when you're sixty-seven years old on a hot summer day, you'll go for that Blizzard-of-the-future, and the change will be in your pocket because what you saved today becomes what you live on tomorrow.

If you are an employee, many companies have programs in which they will deduct savings from your paycheck before you receive it. Now *that's* the best way to beat the savings facade. If you never even see the money you've saved, it doesn't hurt as much to not spend it.

Retirement Plans and Options

People plan for their retirement in many, many different ways. Some save small amounts all along the way. Some trust their employer and Social Security to take care of them. Still others live like misers to save and invest so that they can live like kings when they don't have to work anymore.

The bad news is your retirement will not take care of itself. Social Security has definite limits. Pensions are precarious and much less popular from a corporate point of view. So, retirement, in the end, is like every other area, whether it's your health, your business, or your kid's education. . . you can't just leave it up to the professionals anymore. You need to be hands on if you want to make sure you are taken care of.

The good news is that as the baby boomers have aged they have gotten organized about this being-ready-for-retirement stuff. There are a lot of plans for saving and investing that you can take advantage of here and now to get ready for the someday-sooner-than-you-think. Here are a few of them.

Tax-Deferred Accounts

Do you know what "tax-deferred" accounts are? They are places to store your money so that you won't be taxed on it *for the time being*. They are places that appear on your tax form *before* you get to the taxable income line and go to those tables in the back. Tax-deferred is almost always a very good thing.

But, tax-deferred is not the same as "tax-free." When your tax is deferred, it is only put off until you withdraw the money from the account. Tax-deferred is

A TRUCKLOAD OF CLUES

Watch Out!

Here are some pitfalls you might face on your way to a healthy and happy retirement:

- **Inflation.** Remember when you are planning that what an orange costs today will not be what an orange costs in ten years.

- **Procrastination.** It feels good to put it off until tomorrow, but a bunch of tomorrows only means way too much time spent on other things and a big gulp when retirement reality hits.

- **Catastrophes.** The best-laid plans seldom take into account the tragedies of life, the deaths, the damages, the financial distresses. Think "emergency fund."

- **Inflexibility.** Whatever you were raised to believe about money and finances and retirement options is probably passé now. Your parents faced a different retirement than you will face. Get with the program. Understand how things work and be open to new developments.

- **Underestimating life expectancy.** While we still lose far too many people to disease and accidents, it is still true that people are living longer. Are you planning to provide for yourself for the rest of your life? Are you sure?

- **Leaving it to someone else.** You can't trust a financial pro, a pension plan, or a Social Security deduction to take care of you in your old age. You have to provide for yourself.

- **Failing to talk to everyone involved.** Starting with your spouse and then your kids and then your extended family and friends—talk to the people that will be affected by your plans. Remember that they don't always know what your hopes and dreams are because they are busy living their own lives.

better than taxed, but tax-free is better than tax-deferred.

Here are the questions you want to ask about a tax-deferred account:

* What percentage will the penalty (taxes) be when I withdraw the money?

* Are there any ways to increase or decrease the penalty?

* Will the penalty be based on my original contribution, or will it include the interest earned on that investment?

* Are there different ways to structure this account that will affect either my interest rate or my penalties?

* What are the penalties if I take the money out early?

Annuities

An annuity is a fund. An annuity is a payment. An annuity fund is one that you pay into and then receive payments from. For instance, you can invest $10,000 (you most often *have* to invest at least $5,000) and be guaranteed annuity payments (monthly or yearly) for the rest of your life. Sounds great, doesn't it?

Well, it is good, but you have to be careful to make sure it is great. Annuities are popular because you do one thing, and then you don't have to think about it again. You make that investment, and then you get an

THE BOTTOM LINE

Three Main Kinds of Annuities. . .

Immediate Annuities:
Typically you pay a lump sum of $5,000 or more and immediately begin to receive monthly income for your lifetime, and if defined in the agreement, the lifetime of your spouse.

Deferred Variable Annuities:
Investing in mutual funds through a lump sum or series of payments, but the earnings are tax-deferred until you retire.

Deferred Fixed-Rate Annuities:
These work like certificates of deposit (CDs). You make an investment that is guaranteed a certain interest rate for a certain amount of years.

amount. By the time you retire, that agreed-upon amount may or may not be what you need, but by then it's a done deal.

As with any proverbial coin, there are two sides. The convenience of an annuity is the danger of it. You give up control. You give that initial investment, and then how that investment is handled is totally out of your hands. And it's not that you'll get less than you agreed upon. It's the possibility that your initial investment money possibly could be bringing in much more. Unless you really dig, you can miss a lot of important details about annuities. Much of your money can be eaten up in fees. Much of it can be held because any kind of withdrawal requires a large penalty.

The bottom line is that they (whatever organization you invest in) can take your money and invest it any way they choose. But no matter how wisely they invest it and how much money they make from your investment, they only have to pay you the agreed-upon amount. You might be satisfied with that, but perhaps you should be asking yourself, "If they can invest my money and make more, why don't I just invest my money and make more?"

With the variety of mutual funds and investment options open to you these days, you need to use that old fine-tooth comb to determine for certain whether an annuity is really the way to make the most out of your retirement investment or not.

401(k)

Many companies provide a plan whereby you can invest part of your paycheck (before taxes are applied) toward your retirement. Some companies then match or add to the money that you set aside up to a certain amount (often around 5 percent of your total salary).

There will be a limit to how much money you can invest in your 401(k). Usually that limit is defined by a percentage of your salary or a maximum set by government regulation.

You can often borrow from your own 401(k). If you do, you are charged a percentage of interest that is often a larger percentage than what you are currently earning, but you are paying the percentage to yourself, so it doesn't hurt as much. Remember, though, that if you resign from the company, your loan to yourself is usually due in full. (You always have to count the cost when you borrow money—even from yourself.)

The 401(k) plans were the first of their kind and are the most popular, but there are other plans that have similar functions:

❀ SEPs (Simplified Employee Pensions often used by small companies, sole proprietors, or the self-employed)

❀ 403Bs (often used by nonprofit organizations)

❀ 457 plans (often used by government agencies)

All these plans differ in their terms and conditions, but their basic premise is the same: Take money out before taxes (tax-deferred) and let it start growing toward your retirement. Eventually you'll pay taxes, but not until your money has worked for you just as hard as it possibly can.

Company Pension or Defined Benefit Plans

Every company's pension plan works a little differently, and you don't have a lot of say in this. When you are hired, this kind of plan is laid out for your benefit and information. Don't overlook these documents.

A basic scenario would work this way. When you retire, your pension is doled out to you according to a formula that includes these categories:

❈ Your years of service

❈ Some kind of average salary. They might average your five highest years, or they might average all your years together.

❈ Some percentage to multiply by, usually 1 to 2 percent

Your company, using their version of "the formula," will figure your benefit and begin distributing it to you upon retirement. Often you have to be at the company a certain amount of time before you are fully eligible for this program (fully "vested").

If you are considering retiring early, don't just look at what you will get in your pension—also project what you would have gotten if you'd stayed. A few years can make a bigger difference than you think.

Pension plans are becoming less popular with the advent of plans like the 401(k), but they are still around and you might just be on your way to being vested in one.

IRAs

A Roth IRA is one type of "individual retirement account." It is $3,000 of after-tax money (or $3,500 if age 50 or over) per year that people can tuck away for retirement. It may not be as powerful as a 401(k), but it is every man's retirement plan because anybody, as long as they have earned at least $3,000 that year, can tuck away that $3,000 into an interest-bearing account and let it start to work for them.

The good news about Roth IRAs is you will not be taxed on any money and interest you've earned when you finally withdraw it. The reason most individuals shy away from making this savings commitment is that you are unable, in most situations, to withdraw the money until at least 59½ without incurring a substantial penalty. But if you are willing to wait, the advantages of paying no tax on any realized earnings makes this worth the wait.

A Traditional IRA is $3,000 per year that people can tuck away into a tax-deferred account (with some restrictions) for their retirement. The bad news about Traditional IRAs is you will still be taxed on the money and interest you've earned when you finally withdraw it. The good news is that because your IRA is tax-deferred during the saving process, you will save more money because you aren't taking taxes out and lowering the principal every year.

An IRA is not one certain kind of investment out there waiting for you to find it. IRAs can take the form of many different kinds of investments like mutual funds, stocks, bonds, and CDs.

What's Left for Posterity

The legal stuff: planning your estate. Does it bother you? Does it seem unimportant? Does it make your skin crawl to think about your own life and death?

Part of being financially responsible is having an orderly estate. Part of having an orderly estate is having a formal, legally contractual documentation for how that estate should be handled or distributed when you die or are unable to manage the estate.

What is your estate, you ask? It's the sum total of all your stuff: belongings, objects, property, accounts, money. Does it seem like you don't even have an estate? It won't until something happens to you and someone else has to sort through whatever legal papers they can find of yours in the midst of trying to process the fact that you aren't around anymore. With every letter or call they get from a government agency, your "estate" will seem larger and more fierce to them.

And, in truth, your estate is *your* responsibility, so take responsibility for it and organize it yourself. If you do it now while you think it will be simple, then it will be simpler as you age and accumulate and buy and sell and have kids who have kids, etc.

Here are the main components that are usually discussed when someone talks about your estate. . . .

Your Will

Your will is basically a document that outlines your assets and how you want those assets distributed upon your death. Yes, you can do a will without an attorney. But understand that a will really is a legal document. For that reason, it is money well spent to have a legal professional handle it. (As every lawyer will ask, you wouldn't fix your plumbing yourself, would you? Why would you draw up legal contractual agreements yourself?)

Your will should include an outline of what your estate includes. It also should include an executor, or person who is responsible to see the will carried out. (Let this person know before you name him or her as executor.) Finally, it also should include guardians for any minors who are your responsibility. For this reason, many people draw up their first wills when they have children so that they know that they have cared for their children in the event of their deaths.

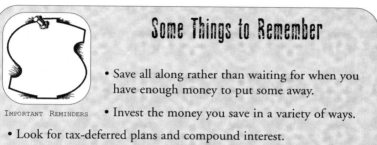

Some Things to Remember

IMPORTANT REMINDERS

- Save all along rather than waiting for when you have enough money to put some away.
- Invest the money you save in a variety of ways.
- Look for tax-deferred plans and compound interest.
- Update your expectations of retirement as you live and age and understand your life more. It's not always just a party for old people.

Your Insurance

You probably have insurance of some kind, even if it's just a small policy attached to your health insurance. Keep your policies up-to-date and keep your papers in a place where your family will be able to find them. There can be a lot of expenses in a prolonged illness or a death. Losing you, as you are, would be hard enough—don't force your family to sort through legal documents and scrape together finances at such a difficult time.

Even if you are single, have a small policy that will cover any burial/funeral expenses. This is a way in which you take care of your family even when you are gone.

Your Power of Attorney

Whom do you want to make decisions for you if you are incapacitated in some way? Is it your spouse? Your brother? You can grant the power of attorney (POA) to this person and be done with it. You can grant them total power of attorney, or you can grant them power of attorney if and when certain circumstances arise such as health problems or your admittance into a nursing home, etc.

Your Living Will

Your living will lets your wishes be known if you should face a situation in which you could be kept alive only by artificial means. A living will is not a "Do Not Resuscitate" statement, but it can include such a statement if you want it to. Living wills are different for each state. Ask at your local hospital; they should have the necessary forms. Let your loved ones know now how you would like them to handle these tough decisions if you are struggling between life and death. They are going to want to do for you what you want them to do. Think about the unthinkable, and let them know your guidelines for your own life and eventual death.

Glossary

401(k)—A retirement plan offered to employees by a company. Contributions are typically tax-deferred.

Asset—Property, such as stocks, homes, cars, savings, etc., that is owned by someone. In the stock market, assets include stocks, bonds, and mutual funds.

Bond—A government-issued note that acts as a loan to the government from the buyer.

Capital Gain Tax—The tax assessed by the government on the income received on an investment.

Commission—The amount of money paid to a broker upon the execution of a purchase or sale of stocks or funds.

Common Stock—A security bought by an investor.

Diversification—Buying several stocks in different sectors attempting to reduce the potential risk.

Dividend—Money paid to a stockholder resulting from the profits of a company.

Dollar Cost Averaging—Buying stocks or funds at regular intervals, resulting in an average purchase price.

Equity Investment—Buying stock with cash rather than with margin (borrowed) money.

Financial Advisor—A professional financial planner who offers advice on investing and other money strategies, often for a commission or flat fee.

Growth Stock—A stock that is expected to rise in price over a given period of time.

Income Stock—A stock that pays dividends that are paid directly to the investor.

IRA—Stands for "Individual Retirement Account." There are several types of IRAs including Roth, tax-deductible, and tax-free.

Margin—A loan offered by an investment firm giving an investor more cash with which to buy stocks.

Market Capitalization—The number of stocks multiplied by the price of each share.

Mutual Fund—A combination of stocks brought together to make a fund, managed by a fund manager.

Net Asset Value (NAV)—The value of a mutual fund after expenses have been deducted multiplied by the number of shares outstanding.

P/E Ratio—The ratio of a company's stock price to its earnings per share.

Principal—The initial amount invested in a stock or fund.

Prospectus—A booklet or report containing the information of a mutual fund. It contains the fund's goals, assets, investments, and yearly earnings statements.

SEP—Stands for "Simplified Employee Pension." A pension plan available to employees of small businesses or to the self-employed. Both employee and employer make contributions.

Stock Dividend—Stocks paid to a shareholder instead of money.

Treasury Bond—A security issued by the government for seven years.

Yield—Money paid on a bond divided by the price of the bond.

Resources for Further Enlightenment

The Money Jungle

We don't expect that the resource you're holding will be the final word in your life on handling your money. So, we want to give you a list of resources that will help you on your journey through the money jungle.

Magazines and Newspapers

Next time you're in the library, check out these magazines and newspapers.

* *Kiplinger's*
* *Forbes*
* *Business Week*
* *Money*
* *Wall Street Journal*
* *Investor's Business Daily*
* *Fortune*
* *Financial Times*
* *Your Money*
* *Family Money*
* *Individual Investor*
* *Worth*

Web Pages

Next time you're surfing, check out these places for online research.

* www.motleyfool.com—Provides basic philosophical information about investing.

* www.moneycentral.msn.com—An excellent site for watching the market and for getting inside information on how the market works and what fuels the market.

* www.hoovers.com—Another site for online research. Comprehensive and filled with both basic and advanced information.

* www.cbs.marketwatch.com/news—A site like msn.com, with a different angle.

* www.nasdaq.com—If you're looking for interesting, in-depth information about the Nasdaq, this site is for you.

- ❀ www.dowjones.com—Like the Nasdaq Web page, this site gives you a broad look at the inner workings of the Dow Jones.

- ❀ www.money.cnn.com—This site has an extensive list of articles geared toward both the new and experienced investor. It also has an especially long list of basic money-related articles.

Online Banks

Gomez Advisors recently scored many of the online banks. Here are some of their top recommendations (for more info on their scoring techniques, surf over to www.gomez.com).

- ❀ Security First Network Bank—www.sfnb.com

- ❀ Wells Fargo Online—www.wellsfargo.com

- ❀ NetBank—www.netbank.com

- ❀ First Internet Bank—www.firstib.com

- ❀ Bank One—www.bankone.com

- ❀ Citibank—www.citibank.com

- ❀ Huntington Bank—www.huntington.com

Online Investing

According to money.com, these are the top online brokerage firms. For more information on their survey and the individual ratings of each company, go to www.money.cnn.com.

- ❀ www.Schwab.com

- ❀ www.csfb.com

- ❀ www.RushTrade.com

- ❀ www.Etrade.com

- ❀ www.Fidelity.com

- ❀ www.Quick-Reilly.com

- ❀ www.Scottrade.com

- ❀ www.Waterhouse.com

- ❀ www.online.msdw.com

❀ www.ABWatley.com

❀ www.Ameritrade.com

❀ www.Brownco.com

Books
So, ya wanna read more, do ya? Try these books for more enlightenment.

❀ Brenner, Lynn & Mark Matcho, *Smart Questions to Ask Your Financial Advisers.* Bloomberg Press, 1997.

❀ Clements, Jonathan, *25 Myths You've Got to Avoid if You Want to Manage Your Money Right.* Simon and Schuster, 1999.

❀ Daskaloff, Alexander, *Credit Card Debt: Reduce Your Financial Burden in Three Easy Steps.* Avon books, 1999.

❀ Gallea, Anthony & William Patalon, *Contrarian Investing.* New York Institute of Finance, 1998.

❀ Gerlach, Douglas, *Investors Web Guide: Tools and Strategies for Building Your Portfolio.* Ziff Davis Press, 1997.

❀ *How to Insure Your Income: A Step-by-Step Guide to Buying the Coverage You Need at Prices You Can Afford.* Silver Lake Publishing, 1997.

❀ Iwaszko, Knute & Brian O'Connell, *The 401(k) Millionaire.* Villard Books, 1999.

❀ Pollack, Kenan & Eric Heighberger, *The Real Life Investing Guide.* McGraw Hill, 1997.

❀ Powers, Mike, *The 21st Century Investor: Investing for Your Child's College Education.* Avon Books, 1998.

❀ Reid, Lisa, *Raising Kids with Just a Little Cash.* Ferguson Carol Publishing, 1996.

❀ Rye, David, *1001 Ways to Save, Grow, and Invest Your Money.* Career Press, 1999.

❀ Schumaker, Ward & Janet Bamford, *Smarter Insurance Solutions.* Bloomberg Press, 1996.

Books (Christian Perspective)
Inexpensive copies of out-of-print books may be found at www.abebooks.com or www.alibris.com.

❀ Alcorn, Randy, *Money, Possessions, and Eternity.* Tyndale House, 2003.

* Blue, Ron, *Taming the Money Monster: Five Steps to Conquering Debt.* Focus on the Family, 1993.

* Blue, Ron and Judy Blue, *Money Matters for Parents and Their Kids.* Thomas Nelson, 1988.

* Blue, Ron and Judy Blue, *Money Talks and So Can We: How Couples Can Communicate about Spending and Giving, Getting Out of Debt, Investing, Planning for Retirement and Other Money Matters.* Zondervan, 1999.

* Blue, Ron and Judy Blue, *Raising Money-Smart Kids: How to Teach Your Children the Secrets of Earning, Saving, Investing, and Spending Wisely.* Thomas Nelson, 1992.

* Burkett, Larry, *Debt-Free Living: How to Get Out of Debt (and Stay Out).* Northfield, 2001.

* Burkett, Larry, *Family Budgets That Work.* Tyndale House, 1988.

* Burkett, Larry, *Family Financial Workbook: A Family Budgeting Guide.* Moody, 2002.

* Dayton, Howard, *Your Money Counts: The Biblical Guide to Earning, Spending, Saving, Investing, Giving, and Getting Out of Debt.* Tyndale House, 1997.

* Pryor, Austin, *Sound Mind Investing: A Step-by-Step Guide to Financial Stability and Growth* (Rev. Ed.). Sound Mind Investing, 2001.

Christian Web Sites

* www.cfnnow.com—Christian Financial Network; a comprehensive site.

* www.christianet.com—ChristiaNet, the Worldwide Christian Marketplace. Links to Christian financial, insurance, and legal resources.

* www.crown.org—Crown Financial Ministries (Larry Burkett); "Teaching People God's Financial Principles."

* www.epm.org—Eternal Perspective Ministries (Randy Alcorn). Includes twenty-seven excellent articles about the biblical perspective on various money matters.

* www.nacfc.org—National Association of Christian Financial Consultants; Web site includes a directory of consultants for specific localities. Members have to submit character references and pastoral recommendations before acceptance into the NACFC.

❀ www.soundmindinvesting.com—A financial newsletter for today's Christian family. Advertised as the "Web's leading source of unbiased investing advice from a biblical perspective."

❀ www.thegoodsteward.com—Online stewardship support center with links to Biblical Principles, Life Stewardship, Financial Matters, etc.

❀ www.timothyplan.com—The Timothy Plan is a family of mutual funds which avoids investing in companies that are involved in practices contrary to Judeo-Christian principles. They state that they are "America's first pro-life, pro-family, biblically-based mutual fund group."